BLACK UTOPIA

BLACK UTOPIA

THE HISTORY OF AN IDEA FROM BLACK NATIONALISM TO AFROFUTURISM

ALEX ZAMALIN

Columbia University Press *New York*

Columbia University Press
Publishers Since 1893
New York Chichester, West Sussex
cup.columbia.edu

A complete CIP record is available from the Library of Congress.
ISBN 978-0-231-18740-4 (cloth)
ISBN 978-0-231-18741-1 (paper)
ISBN 978-0-231-54725-3 (ebook)
LCCN 2019009399

Columbia University Press books are printed on permanent
and durable acid-free paper.
Printed in the United States of America

Cover image: © 2018 Heirs of Aaron Douglas / Licensed by VAGA
at Artists Rights Society (ARS), NY
Corcoran Collection (museum purchase and partial gift from
Thurlow Evans Tibbs, Jr., the Evans–Tibbs Collection),
National Gallery of Art, Washington

Cover design: Lisa Hamm

For Alison, Sam, and Anita

CONTENTS

ACKNOWLEDGMENTS

This book would have been impossible with the ongoing support of many people. I would like to thank my editor, Wendy Lochner, who continues to provide encouragement for my work, and all of the wonderful people at Columbia University Press, whose thoughtfulness and dedication vastly improved the finished manuscript. I would also like the anonymous reviewers who took time out of their schedule to sharpen its scope and final arguments. To my colleagues and students at University of Detroit Mercy—thanks for giving me an opportunity to share my ideas, and for providing many in return. In particular, I would like to thank Michael Barry, Max Burkey, Erin Dwyer, Mike Doan, Joanne Lipson Freed, James Freed, Arthur Getman, Ami Harbin, Mary-Catherine Harrison, Michelle Jacobs, Jon Keller, Matt Kirkpatrick, Kevin Laam, Stephen Manning, Susan McCarty, Dave Merolla, Genevieve Meyers, Mark Navin, Nicholas Rombes, Rosemary Weatherston, and Rodger Wyn. Thanks, as always to, my extended family—Grace Hamilton, Frona Powell, Ron Powell, Aaron Powell, Liz Powell, Arnold Zamalin, Marina Zamalin, Emil Zamalin, and Raya Zamalin. Finally, this book was only possible because of the love of my family. To Alison, Sam, and Anita, thanks for being a constant light in my life, and for always being there.

INTRODUCTION

Utopia and Black American Thought

Black American reflections on the idea of utopia contain some of the most powerful political ideas in the American tradition. Black utopians and antiutopians detailed new visions of collective life and racial identity. They outlined futuristic ways of being. They warned about the disastrous ways of contemporary life, while espousing radical notions of freedom. They speculated on the ideal conditions for fulfilling human desire, while exploding its extant meanings. Human potential was given a new lease on life. Justice was transfigured. They theorized what was scientifically improbable and a new black citizen that seemed impossible.

But reflections on utopia contained a competing impulse. Emancipatory ideas blinded utopians and antiutopians to investments in hierarchy. The wish to create a new world stifled the messy process of democratic deliberation and critical self-examination. Sometimes power became intoxicated upon its own license. And fear roamed undeterred.

Perhaps because of this, we are told today that utopian thought should be dismissed. For critics, it is either politically immature or morally dangerous. It should therefore be placed in the dustbin of history. *Black Utopia* makes an opposing argument. Through

FIGURE 0.1 Sir Thomas More

an intellectual history of its major defenders and critics, it insists that combining black utopia's unseen transformative possibilities with an awareness of its limitations can invigorate contemporary political thinking.

We live in dark times. Ethnonationalism, xenophobia, and racism are on the rise globally. Environmental collapse is around the corner. Economic inequality remains unabated. The threat of armed conflict and war is real. Rather than retreat from reflections on black utopia, now is precisely the time to excavate it for its forgotten vision.

UTOPIA IN HISTORY

The term *utopia* suffers from excessive familiarity.[1] In common usage, it names anything that seems too idealistic. Utopia is, in other words, something that is embraced at youth but abandoned at maturity.[2] But few understand utopia's intellectual lineage. As a radical act of philosophical speculation, utopia coincides with the birth of Western political thought. Some may be familiar with Sir Thomas More's literary masterpiece *Utopia* (1516), which richly described a highly planned society so unreal that it gives u-topia its meaning as a no-place. Others may know something about Francis Bacon's novel *New Atlantis* (1627), which depicted it as one of the mind—of the beauty of intellectual advancement and scientific knowledge. If a perfectly planned space or idea has been integral to utopia's life, nineteenth-century utopian socialists like Robert Owen, Charles Fourier, and Saint-Simon made utopia about repairing a suffering body. For them, the solution was a healthy society—intentional communities that minimized the degrading perils of unjust industrial work. Despite being decried as unscientific and unaware of historical class struggle by Karl Marx and Friedrich Engels in *The Communist Manifesto* (1848), utopia even found its way into their communist society, where each could live according to their abilities and needs. The figure of the ghost that, they said, was "haunting Europe" and was used ironically to express ruling-class fears of communism became quite real in their unwillingness to articulate what a society without class antagonism would entail.

Modern utopian texts had their forbearer in the first major text of the Western tradition, Plato's *Republic*. It told the shadow dwellers of the Athenian city that those who had seen the sun knew that justice was possible only if three classes—the philosopher kings, guardians, and workers—achieved an organic division of intellectual and physical labor and philosophers ruled through reason. Yet even nonutopians couldn't fully escape utopia's presence in their thought. Consider Thomas Hobbes's indivisible authoritarian system of government in *Leviathan*, Jean-Jacques Rousseau's general will, Immanuel Kant's universal history with the cosmopolitan purpose of lasting peace, or Emma Goldman's anarchist defense of community without a state.[3]

Some utopians deny their utopianism. And Americans are perhaps the most egregious in this. One of the American political tradition's founding myths—from *The Federalist* papers to the US Constitution, from Lincoln's civic republicanism to twentieth-century progressivism—is its antiphilosophical, purely political worldview. Americans are far too serious for their own good, so this argument goes, privileging the pragmatic stuff of statesmen grappling with real politics rather than European experiments in metaphysics.[4] Deliberation about the meaning of the Constitution, the framework for governance (as the political theorist Hannah Arendt famously declared), was what made Americans political thinkers par excellence.[5]

But all knee-jerk aversions should raise red flags. They are usually defensive rather than descriptive. After all, America never escaped utopianism: utopianism was integral to its name. Calling the nation "America," as opposed to its proper geographic area of the United States, gestured toward some futuristic transcendent civic religion. American political culture would be defined through a democratic ideology and a belief in exceptionalism. And both myths inspired the conviction of individualistic upward mobility. This mythology was so powerful it convinced people they could do better and otherwise.

This faith was at least part of the reason utopian intentional communities sprang up in the United States from the nineteenth century onward—the Shakers, Oneida community, Twin Oaks, the Farm. More often than not, these were small-knit enclaves organized around socialist economic ideas or countercultural familial organizations. And these ideas constituted a literature too: Edward Bellamy's socialist utopia in *Looking Backward* (1888), Charlotte Perkins Gilman's pacifist feminist society in *Herland* (1915), H. G. Wells's elite-run communist world in *A Modern Utopia* (1905), and Ursula Le Guin's *The Dispossessed* (1974), an otherworldly exploration of the struggle between the soul of capitalist patriarchy and anarcho-communism.[6]

Ultimately, the list of utopian thought is endless, knows no ideology, and is, in the final analysis, a matter of perspective. It captures everything from the religious images evident in the Garden of Eden before the fall from grace and Moses's redemptive rule over the Jews in Exodus to contemporary right-wing faith in free markets and government deregulation. Nonetheless, what unites virtually all utopian thought is the conviction in an ideal society that diminishes suffering, fully realizes human potential, and pushes the boundaries of what seems possible.[7] Embedded in this dream is hope, which exists in the stuff of daydreams of everyday life—what the German philosopher famously Ernst Bloch called the "spirit" of utopia, where there exists the possibility of realizing a new beginning, a future to come, a society yet unrealized but transformative in its vision. In utopia, Bloch wrote, "a new beginning is posited, and the unlost heritage takes possession of itself; that glow deep inside . . . rises from our hearts, unbroken in spite of everything, from the deepest part, that is, the realest part of our waking dream."[8] Utopians are aware of their herculean task. But rather than maintain fantasies of innocence, many know that dreams can become nightmares and that life is too short and filled with too much injustice to not dream for a better one.[9]

Black Utopia begins with the premise that the major reason utopia is a fruitful site for political theory is precisely that it lives on the precipice of human imagination, beyond the border of the possible. Utopia is a laboratory for our most radical desires and mines the recesses of our darkest longings. As the literary critic Northrop Frye writes, "The utopia is a speculative myth; it is designed to contain or provide a vision for one's social ideas, not to be a theory connecting social facts together."[10] Utopia's landscapes are unfamiliar because they bring into life familiar fantasies. Utopia is like religion not because of the dogmatic theology or secular truths it postulates, but because it conjures powerful, irrepressible, sometimes ecstatic feelings: of salvation, of being at home in the world, and of reconciliation with strife. For this reason, utopia is as fruitful a site from which to test the value of our extant political formulations as it is a horizon toward which we might look to improve our lives.

BLACK UTOPIA: POLITICS AND CULTURE

Perhaps the reason scholars have inadequately explored the concept of utopia in the black American tradition is because much of black American life has been nothing short of dystopian. From the outset, slavery denied black people basic physical mobility and political rights, making their bodies exchangeable commodities to be exploited by the highest bidder. Jim Crow subjected them to the daily rituals of dehumanization, making them the target of white aggression and lynch mob violence. De facto segregation placed them in dire living conditions, while prisons eventually became the site where many would live and die. Some of the most dark science fiction fantasies couldn't do justice to such egregious injustice.

But this paints an incomplete picture. A utopian kernel was, indeed, lodged at the beginning of the black experience.[11] The subjugation of slaves created a transcendent culture in which spirituals embodied the prophetic faith in reaching the promised land of freedom.[12] This utopian strain of hope, based on what are arguably the three pillars of African American political thought (liberation, justice, and freedom), is evident in everything from Frederick Douglass's abolitionist dream of emancipation to Sojourner Truth's feminist ideal of gender equality, from Martin Luther King's vision of a beloved liberal community to contemporary black activists calling for abolishing mass incarceration.

Historically, such hope did, in fact, give rise to various intentional black communities of wide-ranging goals. Some were organized by white benefactors with the aim of cultural uplift, while others were built on the idea of self-sufficiency—whether the runaway maroon slave colonies, or all-black towns like Mound Bayou, in the Mississippi Delta, founded by ex-slaves in 1887.[13]

But utopian hope is not identical with the very space in which it has been most vividly detailed: the theoretical meditation on ideal politics, communities, and identities. The first clear black utopian vision was in the nineteenth-century black nationalist Martin R. Delany. Delany cast black migration to Central America, South America, and Africa as a counterpoint to black disenchantment about slave emancipation. And he dramatized it through a worldwide slave revolt in what was the first work of black fantasy fiction, *Blake; or the Huts of America* (1859). His spirited defense of black self-rule was never fully elaborated. But it would be textured through political novelist intellectuals like Sutton E. Griggs, Frances Harper, Pauline Hopkins, and Edward A. Johnson. Their work dramatized a critical black public that opposed the white supremacy and racial violence defining Jim Crow America.

In the early twentieth century, questions of black self-determination would transform into a meditation on the possibility of a postracist future in which global white supremacy was abolished. W. E. B. Du Bois's short story "The Comet" (1920) asked: How would race matter after the apocalypse? A decade later, his novel *Dark Princess* (1928) visualized the conditions for achieving a Global South utopia, in which all people of color united for collective self-determination. Du Bois's wish, however, couldn't contain his clear-eyed skepticism. And such skepticism was displayed in what was the first major black antiutopian text, George Schuyler's classic satire *Black No More* (1931). There, Schuyler upped the ante on, while dismantling faith in, liberal dreams of racial equality and assimilation. He did this by imagining a condition in which all black Americans could undergo a medical procedure to become physically white. Yet no less biting was Schuyler's *Black Empire* (1938), which countered the idea of black racial purity. *Black Empire*'s fictionalization of an authoritarian black global imperialist movement satirized white myths about black docility. And it challenged conventional wisdom about painless racial reformism.

In the postwar period, amid the various African anticolonial independence movements, meditations on colorblindness and color consciousness were replaced with dreams of decolonization. This was a world in which black people neither cowered to white imperialism nor spoke in political vocabularies that only whites understood. Richard Wright's travelogue of his visit to what was then the Gold Coast colony (now Ghana), *Black Power* (1954), captured his frustration about this possibility. Nonetheless, while *Black Power* was an antiutopian meditation on colonized citizens' inability to escape their colonizer's ways, it outlined a countervailing idealism that Wright himself never fully appreciated.

Black utopia would eventually be redeemed in the 1960s, but by an iconoclastic figure who collapsed the boundary between political theory and aesthetics. The avant-garde jazz musician and poet Sun Ra's life spanned much of the twentieth century, but what he witnessed made him wish to escape its prevailing ideologies. When Ra said he and his philosophy were out of this world, he meant it. Retelling his abduction to Saturn throughout his life was just one example of the way his iconoclastic cosmology blurred the lines between delusion and brilliance. But his philosophy of Afrofuturism said something about the depths of black despair and the possibility of constructing a new citizen.

In the early 1970s, utopia wasn't abandoned. Instead, it was given a critical take through the work of the science fiction writer Samuel R. Delany. His musings on the nexus between identity and desire in *Trouble on Triton: An Ambiguous Heterotopia* (1976) both advanced and problematized radical notions of social freedom. Delany's society of sexual and gender liberation in *Triton* may have been the diametrical opposite of the postapocalyptic dystopia depicted in Octavia E. Butler's novels *Parable of the Sower* (1993) and *Parable of the Talents* (1998). But Butler's work also offered a utopian image—one that was based in a community of hope and resilience, amid growing economic insecurity in a world that resembled late-twentieth-century America.

Some of these figures conjured ideal black societies or examined utopian ideals of American society. Others speculated in fiction about a future in which technology would transform the world. Some fictionalized postapocalyptic events that made utopian change possible. Others rejected the idea of utopia in politics, if not expressing serious antiutopian critiques throughout their work. Still others exquisitely detailed how utopias could become dystopias, and vice versa.

Arguably, all can broadly fit into what the critic Mark Dery has termed the tradition of "Afrofuturism," black American texts that both revise history and imagine impossible trajectories of black freedom. But black utopia is irreducible to Afrofuturism, which has long been associated with science fiction and technology in the future, replete with robots and supercomputers.[14] Indeed, *Black Utopia* argues that if black utopia has been an expression of what the political scientist Richard Iton has called the "black fantastic," it has, as much as anything else, been a fantastical meditation on untapped possibilities already embedded within society—unconditional freedom, equality, interracial intimacy, solidarity, and social democracy.[15]

MODERNITY, COUNTERCULTURE, AND CRITIQUE

Black utopia was never a transhistorical idea. This is because its meaning had everything to do with the existing social conditions of a given moment. But its specific concern was always with the black diaspora. By taking up ideal solutions to the specific problems of slavery, colonialism, Jim Crow, lynching, mass incarceration, deregulation, and war, black utopia was in conversation with prevailing political realities, crises, and cultural trends. Black reflections upon utopia emerged from the Afro-modern experience, which was defined by the experience of enslavement, global empire, and the formative role of Enlightenment idealism and its radical offshoots. This experience is what the critic Paul Gilroy has called the "double-consciousness" of the black Atlantic.[16]

This is why black utopian images ranged from black emigration and interracial solidarity to postracialism, Pan-Africanism, and interplanetary escape into the cosmos. But each reiteration retained shared visions. Black utopians rehashed elements of Platonic idealism about total social transformation, while antiutopians were more critical about its prospects. But utopians were often more self-consciously aware than antiutopians, whose romantic critiques embodied the utopianism they denounced.

What united black utopians and antiutopians was a concern with exploring the hidden dynamics and logical consequences of racism. This distinguished them from their white European counterparts. As ideologies and instruments for developing global capitalism and modern political states, race and white supremacy have been central to modernity. They have created a system of domination in which white skin is valued higher than black skin.[17] One troubling consequence of Euro-modern racism was to excise people of color from the historical record—from the time of political action and from freedom. The philosopher Lewis Gordon summarizes this in the following way: "the appeal to blacks as problem-people is an assertion of their ultimate location outside the systems of order and rationality."[18] This is what the German philosopher G. W. F. Hegel most famously accomplished in his posthumous *Lectures on the Philosophy of History* (1837). In the same text that aimed to explain the evolution of ideas in action throughout time, he relegated Africa to a premodern place in which there was virtually nothing—only a placeholder for the imagination that would expand freedom to all in the nineteenth-century Prussian state. Hegel wrote, "in Africa," "history is out of the question. Life there consists of contingent happenings and surprises. . . . There is no subjectivity, but merely a series of subjects who destroy each other."[19]

Black utopians thus had their work cut out for them. If most utopians in the Western tradition struggled to envision a subject capable of disrupting the flow of political common sense, black utopians needed to seize a space of imagination from which they were barred and imagine a new humanity from which they were excluded. This is why they announced their claims without seeking prior approval, why they mixed different narrative genres, emotional registers, and eclectic theoretical sources in their futuristic visions, and why history and identity became unavoidable sites of inquiry and terrains of engagement.

Black utopians and antiutopians engaged in a unique form of utopian theorizing, unlike that of the European tradition. This is the first overarching contention of this book. They refused what had been common in the Western tradition: to idealize people of color as empty vessels upon which to project their greatest fears and unrealized longings. Without question, some thinkers partook in a civilizational discourse that privileged a capitalist, liberal democratic vision of political development. But their imaginings were usually filled with complex citizens rather than what the eighteenth-century philosopher, Jean-Jacques Rousseau called "noble savages," living in serene conditions. The effect of this was important. The romantic tropes, sense of wholeness, spiritual redemption, and rational teleology that had long been a staple of Western utopia was given a different take in the black tradition. Utopia in black became much more critical and infused by a sense of tragedy. It became defined by unfinished conversations, unresolved debates, critical problematics, which resisted easy resolution. In black utopia, a sense of committed struggle in the face of the unknown was coupled with a realistic sense of subversion and collapse. Substantively, black utopia was envisioned as a future society to be founded in postracism rather than postracialism. Citizens of color were imagined to be free from the fetters of white supremacy and racial violence. But they chose the terms under which they would flourish according to their own desires without white expectations.

The second argument of this book is that reflections upon black utopia were defined by a unique take on perennial questions of political theory. Political rule was debated between the two main poles of Western utopianism—elitism and collective rule. Nineteenth-century utopians were both more optimistic about radical transformation and more elitist in privileging what Du Bois would famously call a politics based on the "talented tenth"—business leaders, intellectuals, and politicians—rather than the masses. But they still retained a critique of arbitrary elite power and implicitly defended citizens' capacity for self-rule. For their part, twentieth-century figures were more vigorous defenders of popular rule, but they stressed its ambiguities. They were especially savvy in understanding the racial terror behind democratic populism—the lynch mobs, vigilantes, night riders, slave catchers. They refused to blindly submit to romantic strains of utopian anarchism or communism that promised equality. Only some had a strong sense of human nature, but both traditions preferred to speak instead of a socially constructed human condition and describe it as far too unwieldy to be domesticated for easy political solutions. Their work accepted certain tenets of modern realism: a perspectival understanding of power, a commitment to pluralism, an awareness of the complex desires animating action. But it also combined this understanding with what realists rejected—belief in the collective popular will, a defense of equality, and a defense of localized knowledge.

Some theorists of utopia embraced organic community. Others held romanticized views of identity, gender, class, and race founded in essentialist notions of identity. But more often than not, their work defended inorganic visions founded in solidarity. Moreover, they engaged in speculative thinking about freedom that eschewed abstract reasoning common to social contract theory. Instead, theoretical reflection became a matter of engaging with lived experience. Black utopians and antiutopians often embodied what the German sociologist Max Weber called the spirit of rationalization and religious disenchantment central to modernity. Nonetheless, they retained elements of spiritualism and transcendence that made politics exceed rationalism.[20]

Moreover, unlike their nineteenth-century utopian counterparts, twentieth-century antiutopians were far more critical of the emancipatory power of the Enlightenment. Antiutopians lamented mechanized instrumental reason, simple progress, and science unchecked by moral authority. This was because they were mindful of the terrors of global war, mass genocide, and the violent legacy of imperialism. But both black utopians and antiutopians together tried to advance an alternative vision to liberation. This was based less on the notion of perfect mastery and instead on a mixture of pragmatic experimentation and critical reexamination. Black utopians were much more drawn to something approximating a critical civic sphere defined around shared collective interests and based on reason. But antiutopians, too, refused to abandon the ideal of truth, while maintaining skepticism about absolute self-certainty and messianic promises. Utopians critiqued power to expose what it concealed and obscured, while remaining committed to a critical form of reason serviceable for collective life. That black utopia was often left unelaborated was less a failure of imagination and more a defense of keeping alive a horizon, which would exist as unfulfilled possibility.

The third argument of this book is that, although escape from US white supremacy was a core theme that united both traditions, there was nothing escapist about their critique of American culture. They demonstrated that American individualism perpetuated a sense of moral apathy, capitalism relied on a logic of exploitation that resembled enslavement, free markets crippled the resources necessary to create basic freedom, self-interest devolved into a crude battle over resources, which resulted in violence, if not war.

Moreover, they repurposed core American political ideas to be serviceable for black liberation. In their work, American realism, which justified practical solutions to concrete political problems, actually became the justification for idealism, which pushed the boundaries of possibility and value. American instrumentalism and means-and-ends thinking became a way to achieve a condition where citizens could be treated as ends rather than means. The critique of law became a justification to start a new polity. Liberal pluralism became the justification for a more experimental politics and freer society.

Black Utopia's overarching claim is that black reflections on utopia express what the historian Wilson J. Moses has understood as a defining characteristic of African American thought: its "creative conflict."[21] Often, the political radicalism of their work (i.e., ideas of popular autonomy, equality, freedom, and total liberation and critiques of authoritarianism and unbridled capitalism) stood in opposition to the antiegalitarian political visions held by some of its authors (elitist denigration of popular authority, the defense of gender domination and patriarchy). This is not surprising. After all, conflict has always been common to utopian thought as such. The experimental desire to begin something new explodes what is real and sensible of a given moment, or what itself counts as the future.

UTOPIA AND THE BLACK AMERICAN POLITICAL TRADITION

What follows is a study of the relationship between culture, politics, and the black imagination, as expressed through the organizing idea of utopia. *Black Utopia*'s choice of texts is motivated less by a particular ideological orientation and more by the centrality with which they examine or articulate utopia. Utopias are as real or ephemeral as utopian thoughts. Sometimes they are hidden in plain sight. Sometimes the dystopian emerges as a hidden utopian. No doubt, black communists, democratic socialists, radical feminists, queer theorists, and a range of other political thinkers drew from the reservoir of a utopian imaginative horizon to make political claims upon society. But more often than not, their primary preoccupation was less with giving vivid texture to an ideal society. It was more with a normative defense of their position and a critique of unjust structures it opposed.[22]

The first reason *Black Utopia*'s focus is primarily on cultural texts rather than political treatises is because this is where utopia was given its fullest expression. Culture has always played a crucial role in the black political imagination because it was rarely given space in the US public sphere. Instead, it emerged in what the political scientist James Scott has called the "hidden transcript."[23] Culture—whether the early slave rituals or later the jazz, blues, literary autobiography, and journalism—forged the contours of black collective identity and strategies of resistance.[24]

The second reason is that the utopian imagination has often been expressed through art. Plato's *Republic* fictionalized dialogues to test philosophical truths. More's *Utopia* used an imagined travel narrative to expand the boundaries of common sense. Marx and Engels's *The Communist Manifesto* combined Shakespearean tragedy and romantic resolution to defend the triumph of the proletariat. In many utopian texts, transformative imagination countered existing realities, which had long been centered on reinforcing extant power structures. And political experiments like socialism, communism, and even nationalism all had a cultural dimension, and were infused by the spirit of romantic possibility and unfulfilled horizon, evident in utopian literature.[25]

Furthermore, black utopia made aesthetics political. This was not because it always addressed matters pertaining to the structure of the state, the allocation of socioeconomic goods. It was because it revised the normative horizon necessary for liberation. Even more strikingly, however, utopia in black was a popular cultural phenomenon, despite its controversial ideas. It was consumed by many readers and serialized in journals and magazines to great fanfare. Black utopia rejected the strict dichotomy between high and low culture that the twentieth-century Frankfurt School critical theorist Theodor Adorno famously articulated as central to a total critique of what he understood as an inverted whole.[26] The melodramatic narrative tone, salacious plots, and hyperbolic characters evident in black utopian and antiutopian literature made political ideas more accessible, even if they were radical.

Methodologically, my concern in *Black Utopia* is not primarily analytical—What exactly makes a black utopian text? How do we classify them? And it is not driven by questions of categorization. For example, are black nationalists or Pan-Africanists utopians or pragmatists? Are liberals or conservatives who discuss utopia in fiction not simply offering a testing ground for their political vision? Though I try to answer these questions along the way, I am more concerned with politics.[27] And many of these texts have only received marginal treatment from political theorists.

Some, like the sociologist Karl Mannheim, have tried to bifurcate all politics into either the "ideological" (the existing thoughts that reinforced a given social system) or the "utopian," which pushes against it and tries to imagine a better future. But this division is too overdetermined and analytically problematic because it reduces all countercultural and radical thought to utopia.[28]

In contrast, *Black Utopia*'s intellectual ambition is to texture and restore to its proper place a neglected site of the black American political and cultural imagination; and it is to offer a critical interpretation of the idea of utopia. Among the questions it answers are, What is the meaning of utopia across time? How does it figure into the tradition of political theory? How does it engage questions common to modernity? What ought to be redeemed or discarded from its legacy? In what ways could utopia energize contemporary thought and practice?[29]

Black Utopia's belief is that answering these questions helps to deepen both the Western tradition of utopian thought and thinking about modernity in general, as well as the black American and American intellectual traditions in particular. Each chapter's goal is to situate a figure in their intellectual and political moment to demonstrate the unseen complexities, possibilities, and limitations of their work and unappreciated dimensions of their thought. The goal is as much to understand the boundaries of the black political and cultural imagination as it is to see what lessons it has for contemporary political life. It is to assess which elements of black utopian and antiutopian thought ought to be reclaimed or abandoned.

1

MARTIN DELANY'S EXPERIMENT IN ESCAPE

The nineteenth-century black emigrationist Martin Robison Delany (1812–85) was an iconoclastic thinker whose work escaped the liberal–conservative divide.[1] At various moments throughout his life, American political reality led Delany to reject the assimilationist position of his coeditor of the *North Star* newspaper, the abolitionist Frederick Douglass, and insist it was a dead-end strategy. Around this time, his mantra was this: "But we must go from among our oppressors; [liberation] never can be done by staying among them."[2] After being dismissed from Harvard Medical School because of racism in 1850, Delany became a forceful proponent of emigration to Central and South America. He moved to Canada in 1856 and by 1859 signed a treaty with Alake of Abeoukuta to have an African American settlement in West Africa. When the Civil War began, Delany joined the Union Army and, when it ended, the Reconstruction effort. But when Reconstruction became a lost cause he began advocating for black emigration to Liberia in the late 1870s, collaborating with the very organization, the American Colonization Society (ACS), he once opposed.

By the end of his life, Delany's conservatism intensified. He supported a white supremacist Democrat, Wade Hampton, in his successful bid for South Carolina governor in 1876. He rejected

FIGURE 1.1 Martin Robison Delany

Radical Republican efforts at redistributing Rebel-held land during Reconstruction. And he insisted that slavery was a civilizing institution, which earned him the admiration of white supremacists and conservatives alike. This led Douglass to see Delany as a defender of the old planter class.

Delany was virtually forgotten for almost a century before being revived in the late 1960s by the Black Power movement. It was then that he became proof blackness was synonymous with resistance. Ever since, debates have centered on the following:

Was he a true nationalist or an American patriot who turned to nationalism as a last resort because he couldn't find acceptance in the United States? Was he a racial essentialist or savvy pragmatist? But situating Delany in the narrow context of debates about black politics, political ideology, and political strategy misses his meditation on the meaning of an ideal black society.[3]

Especially throughout the 1850s, in what became known as his "emigrationist phase," Delany extended to black citizens a vision missing from the nineteenth-century utopian communitarian energy being spread throughout the United States. These were the Shaker colonies and the Phalanx communities inspired by the utopian-socialism of Charles Fourier. In what was both his most famous text and the first black nationalist one, *The Condition, Elevation, Emigration, and Destiny of the Colored People of the United States* (1852), Delany insisted black freedom dreams were stillborn. This was especially the case after the Fugitive Slave Act (1850) nationalized slavery by making runaway slaves subject to retrieval in the north. In what is generally regarded as the first work of black utopian fiction, *Blake; or the Huts of America* (1859),[4] Delany fictionalized a global slave insurrection and Pan-African community. His work imagined what history couldn't: black liberation on black terms.

Black escape to a new world was the first idea of black utopia. The idea was never fully realized or clearly elaborated in Delany's work. But it was glimpsed as a land of economic abundance in which black citizens would be able to achieve dignity through self-sufficiency. What Delany clearly imagined, however, was the way it could be realized: not through quietism or withdrawn individualism, but through collective unsanctioned resistance. Delany was undoubtedly the first theorist of utopia who tested the boundaries of radical claim-making and imagination. But this is also why his work expressed a paradoxical vision. It pushed against the boundaries of American political possibility, even if it often retained vestiges of some political ideas that perpetuated inequality.[5]

AMERICAN INDIVIDUALISM AND RADICAL CRITIQUE

Like many modern utopian texts from the Enlightenment onward, *The Condition* replaced a Christian prophetic strain of reaching a beloved Kingdom of God in some distant future or a prepolitical Garden of Eden of natural harmony with a secular black politics.[6] *Blake* implicated religion in black quietism and Delany thought white Christianity masquerading as benevolence perpetuated slaveholder exploitation. As *Blake*'s protagonist, the ex-slave Henry Blake says, "tell me nothing about religion when the man who hands you bread at the communion, has sold your daughter away from you!"[7] Nonetheless, Delany treated industrial capitalism with the same religious zeal as many Americans of his generation. As he said in *The Condition*:[8]

> Society regulates itself. . . . "Like seeks like," is a principle in the laws of matter, as well as of mind. There is such a thing as inferiority of things, and positions; at least society has made them so; and while we continue to live among men, we must agree to all *just* measures—all those we mean, that do not necessarily infringe on the rights of others. By the regulations of society, there is no equality of attainments.[9]

Though he followed Marx and Engels by leaving unelaborated what utopia would look like and prioritized the importance of political economy over political rights, Delany was no economic egalitarian. Instead, he made American acquisitive individualism applicable to black uplift, and couldn't imagine an idea of equality beyond opportunity.[10] He envisioned freedom as government nonintervention. Social life was a matter of conforming to constraints, not exploding them.[11]

A realistic sense of black limitation amid white supremacy animated Delany's argument about black emigration. This was understandable. But more problematic was his desire to replicate the common sense of the American ruling class in a future black utopian society in which white supremacy would, at least in principle, no longer be a debilitating problem.

Never did Delany propose the kind of pragmatism attempted by one of his contemporaries, the utopian-socialist Robert Owen, who emigrated from England to New Harmony, Indiana, to secure capitalist investment and the tools of industrial production to liberate society from exploitative working conditions. Instead, far from being critical of the enterprise, Delany was awestruck at the marvels capitalism could build—ships, railroads, monuments—without acknowledging what *The Communist Manifesto* (1848) argued several years earlier: that capitalism created mansions for the rich and dilapidated hovels for the working poor.[12] Delany had little concern with economic inequality. Instead, he would repeat in mantra-like fashion, "Let our young men and women prepare themselves for usefulness and business."[13]

But Delany's work outlined an alternative political theory that stood in opposition to these commitments. *The Condition*'s critique of white supremacy extended nineteenth-century utopian critiques of natural elite power and rigid class hierarchy that Delany sometimes uncritically defended within the black community. His justification of collective black self-rule turned on denaturalizing racial inequality as a product of historical political choices. Nothing bothered Delany more than arbitrary power. And in the American legal system he saw its most egregious embodiment. It masqueraded violence, justified inequality, repressed hidden social vulnerability and it defined injustice as justice through excising black citizens from humanity. "The *will* of the man who sits in judgment on our liberty, is the law," he wrote. "To him is given *all power* to say, whether or not we have a right to enjoy freedom."[14] Delany defined racial domination as a product of dialectical power struggle over social identity. This led to the construction of a "policy," where people of color were enslaved because they "had the *least chance*, or [were] the *least potent* in urging their claims."[15]

Delany's theoretical critique of elite power came from his redefinition of racism. It was a strategic choice of the ruling class to fracture interracial solidarity. He claimed that "to ensure the greater success," white elites promoted racism "because it engenders the greater prejudice," and "elicits less interest on the part of the oppressing class, in their favor."[16] This claim opposed the classic American form of racist reasoning, epitomized in Thomas Jefferson's *Notes on the State of Virginia* (1785), which suggested that antiblack racism came from natural white antipathy toward black physical appearance.[17] Moreover, although Delany subscribed to a pluralist view of politics in which factional interests engaged in a self-interested struggle, his critique of white supremacy centralized the disastrous consequences of rational self-interest. He warned that black citizens in the North couldn't depend on white goodwill because when "their own property and liberty are jeopardized . . . they will not sacrifice them for us."[18] This argument resembled that of his contemporary, the transcendentalist critic Ralph Waldo Emerson, who claimed that "each citizen has a view of his own, which, if followed to its extreme, would leave no room for any other citizen."[19] Such a view defined *Blake*. The figure of Major Armsted—like Jefferson—is "morally opposed to slavery" but profits from it as a matter of "self-interest."[20] And Blake's singular desire for solidarity with a slaveholding Choctaw Indian makes him unwilling to forcefully and unequivocally challenge his practice.[21]

FREEDOM, POWER, AND IDENTITY

Delany's Aristotelianism—or his primary concern with what he called "the *practical* application of principles adduced"[22]—exploded American racial common sense about freedom. Delany mobilized modern natural rights and equality claims, which inspired the eighteenth-century republican revolutions in France, the United States, and Haiti and socialist revolutions across the world in 1848. But he did this to make blackness into a force for resistance against arbitrary power. Delany's dethroning of power from its pedestal of invulnerability was most eloquently captured in *Blake*. The slaveholder Colonel Franks's insistence that Blake, a freed slave now returning to purchase his enslaved wife, Maggie, needs to be flogged for publicly disrespecting him is telling. It expressed Delany's belief that power's demonstration betrayed its own confidence. "If slavery is right," Franks tells Blake, "the master is justifiable in enforcing obedience to his will; deny him this, and you at once deprive him of the right to hold a slave."[23] Moreover, Delany's theoretical presumption of black equality opposed the nineteenth-century racist argument about inherent black intellectual and moral inferiority and the legitimacy of unjust law. This animated his argument that "Natural rights may, by virtue of unjust laws, be obstructed, but never can be annulled."[24]

Such a nascent modern egalitarian worldview stood in opposition to Delany's own investment in benevolent male rule. Characterizing women's capacity for social usefulness commendably assaulted narratives of subdued femininity. But it was still tethered to Delany's disregard for the arbitrary gender norms embodied in his lament of a lost masculinity. This contradictory impulse was captured in the following statement:

> Until colored men, attain to a position above permitting their mothers, sisters, wives, and daughters, to do the drudgery and menial offices of other men's wives and daughters; it is useless, it is nonsense, it is pitiable mockery, to talk about equality and elevation in society. The world is looking upon us, with feelings of commiseration, sorrow, and contempt. We scarcely deserve sympathy, if we peremptorily refuse advice, bearing upon our elevation.[25]

An obvious inconsistency existed between *Blake*'s valorization of a revolutionary councilwoman, Madame Cordora, and its presentation of community regeneration through marriage. Very few women are given narrative voice or internal monologues. Women almost always exist in the shadows, or in support of, men—if they are not problematically depicted as too religious, subservient, or hysterical.[26] Like many male figures of his time, Delany was never able to fully appreciate what was sometimes implied in his work and powerfully asserted by his black feminist contemporaries. Indeed, Sojourner Truth, Maria Stewart, Ida B. Wells, and Anna Julia Cooper understood that black women's subordination under patriarchy was incommensurable with a commitment to equality and derailed collective black freedom dreams.

But at other times, *Blake* rejected the image of black political passivity across the gender line asserted through the abolitionist

Harriet Beecher Stowe's best-selling novel *Uncle Tom's Cabin* (1852), to which it was a direct literary response. *Blake* claimed black resistance required seizing unsanctioned political claims, rather than what *Uncle Tom's Cabin* sought to accomplish: fomenting abolitionist white sentiment through simplistic accounts of black suffering. *Blake*'s thesis is crystallized in the dialogue between Blake and Cordora when he arrives in Havana, Cuba:

> "And these are really the people declared by American laws, to 'have no rights that a white is bound to respect'? Why have we so long submitted to them?" said the Madame with a burst of indignation, taking her seat amidst demonstrations of intense emotion. . . . "And if we say it shall, it will be so!" added Madame Cordora . . . "Then it shall be so!" declared Blake. "Then," concluded Madame, "it will be so."[27]

Laws can restrict freedom and brutalize bodies, but they cannot squash sovereign mind. Intention creates imagination, which becomes articulated through speech. Verbal utterances give nascent political ideas reality to the speaker, who is no longer seized by hampering doubts of their impossibility. Awareness of one's autonomy and political freedom are analytically distinct. But the first is often a precondition for the second.

Without question, Delany himself embraced Eurocentric theories of progress. This was expressed through his preoccupation with thinking about emigration through considering the question of natural resources, political dynamics, and demographics found in Canada, Central America, and South America. But Delany rejected the idea that black autonomy depended upon realizing political rights or socioeconomic resources. Despite insisting upon the importance of exemplary political action through the mold of Platonic elites equipped with virtue, Delany extended to ordinary black people what G. W. F. Hegel called the "master-slave" dialectic and what became Marx and Engels's justification for working-class popular rule.[28] The constant theme throughout Delany's work was that oppression created the condition for liberation. Everyday work on the plantation—planting rice, tobacco farming, cotton picking—was the way dominated black people recognized and exhibited their capacity for self-governance: "the blacks themselves are the only skillful cultivators—the proprietor knowing little or nothing about the art."[29] This created a condition of revolutionary fearlessness. As *Blake*'s narrator puts it, "the blacks have everything to hope for and nothing to fear. . . . They must and will be free; whilst the whites have everything to fear and nothing to hope for."[30] Indeed, Delany's defense of individualism captured an unexpected philosophical vision. The hands forced to labor unjustly were the hands that could remake the world in a different image: "Our elevation must be the result of *self-efforts*, and work of our *own hands*."[31]

Although late in life he subscribed to the discredited idea that black political ineptitude led to the failure of Reconstruction, throughout the 1850s Delany decolonized freedom by unmooring it from the requirement of reasonable expectations and acculturation. He refused the developmental perspective exemplified in *Blake* through the Cuban revolutionary poet Placido, who says, "we have much yet to learn to fit us for freedom." Blake's response to this position was also Delany's: "we know enough now. . . . All that remains to be done, is to make ourselves free."[32] Delany's delinking of black freedom from white reasoning was what explained his call for black citizens to lead the abolitionist movement. And it accounted for his problem with the American Colonization Society, which tried to reinforce white benevolence while limiting experiments in black self-governance.[33] But by connecting freedom's realization to the vivid imagination of its dreamers, Delany made it more difficult to be monopolized by the narrow dreams of the elite—the black bourgeoisie, military leaders, elected officials, and cultural leaders, groups of which he was, at times, part. This was the meaning behind Blake's assertion that "Our ceremonies . . . originated by ourselves, adopted to our own condition, circumstances, and wants, . . . [will be realized] as impressed upon the tablet of each of our hearts."[34]

Relatedly, although Delany's Aristotelian equation of moral virtue with exemplary citizenship in *The Condition* justified the patriotic activities of distinguished black citizens, it also had the effect of untethering citizenship from noble birth. The logical implication of his overarching thesis that, "having made the greatest investments, [citizens] necessarily have the greatest interests"[35] was that future black community was to be created through action, not something that existed prepackaged in advance. Black people who worked on the polity were its true members, not the violent slave masters or the white racist abolitionists, who used black bodies as instruments to enrich their lives, to assuage self-doubt, to feel invincible.

In *Blake*, Delany connected this point to freedom. The word *freedom* appears only a dozen times over the course of three hundred pages. But one of its clearest appearances is in the narrator's description of the streets of New Orleans, where, upon arrival, Blake is transfixed and mesmerized by

> a fashionable young white lady of French or American extraction, and there the handsome and frequently beautiful maiden of African origin, mulatto, quadroon, or sterling black, all fondly interchanging civilities. . . . Freedom seemed as though for once enshielded by her sacred robes and crowned with cap and wand in hand, to go forth untrammelled through the highways of

> town. . . . [One could see] many a creole, male or female, black, white, or mixed race . . . in sentimental reflection on some pleasant social relation, or sad reminiscence of ill-treatment or loss by death of some loved one, or worse than death, the relentless and insatiable demands of slavery.[36]

Not only is interracial community revealed as beautiful, but it is the closest thing to a classic utopian society of organic harmony in the entire book. This vision was diametrically opposed to what later critics would remember most about *Blake*—its sensationalized unfinished conclusion, in which the final words detail the Grand Council announcing violent race war against whites.[37] Indeed, this conclusion had everything to do with a militant rhetoric that Delany thought would move black people to resist, rather than *Blake*'s overarching narrative.

Blake was a novel not about the necessity of violent war, but about the ambiguities of creating an ideal polity where difference of opinion was to be managed, competing interests debated, the good life articulated, and political tactics developed. Blake's journey—from the Deep South to Cuba, which led to slave insurrection in plantations, closed quarters, back alleys, streets, towns, and cities to destroy racial domination—dramatized a powerful idea: Community is defined through collective negotiation of the joys and terrors of social interaction, not through settled answers and decrees, through communication not blood. Identity is made through choices, not a fixed history. Desire and interests are too fluid to be stabilized. Confusion, ambiguity, and intermixture are to be embraced.

Blake's image of performance and interracial intimacy stood in opposition to a competing one Delany defended later in life. In his last work, *Principa of Ethnology: The Origin of Races and Color* (1880), the political choices Delany emphasized in the construction of racial difference in *The Condition* were obscured. This was evident in his account of a prepolitical, skin-based theory of black identity based on "rouge" skin pigmentation, and through his theological narrative about how God created three distinct races from one blood—Ham (black), Shem (yellow), and Japheth (white).[38] Nonetheless, Delany's arguments were never about solidifying racial hierarchy, but about reversing popular racist scientific accounts of black inferiority. Central to this was his theory of "monogenesis," the idea that all human beings equally descended from one origin.[39] Furthermore, by explaining racial differences through a biblical story, he made race into a socially constructed narrative that required ex post facto justification rather than an unchangeable truth. Race became a story that required a beginning, middle, and end. *Principa* thus laid the philosophical groundwork for countering the racial essentialism that *Blake* rendered culturally and politically unsustainable. Delany thus linked identity to cultural production rather than skin-color—as difference without hierarchy—and turned it into a narrative. He did this even if he never renounced his problematic view that miscegenation was unnatural, when he said, "miscegenation . . . cannot take place. . . . The works of God [would] be set at naught, his designs and purposes thwarted."[40]

Delany's meditations on black resettlement were as complex as his views on race. His anticipation of Western European imperialist designs on Africa led him to abandon his plan in 1861 to relocate to the Niger Valley in Liberia. But his fascination with the utopian theme of discovery blinded him to the possibility of cultural imperialism. "Go with the fixed intention—as Europeans come to the United States," he told would-be black American explorers, "of cultivating the soil, entering into the mechanical operations, keeping of shops, carrying on merchandise, trading on land and water, improving property."[41] Delany often ignored the citizens of Central America, South America, and Niger, who, like Native Americans, neither asked for nor wanted what generations of immigrants were compelled to embrace in the United States—the ideology of upward mobility, rational self-interest, and capitalist industrialization. Throughout *The Official Report of the Niger Valley Exploring Party* (1861), Delany was clearly mired in his cultural provincialism. He was uninterested in thinking about how non-Western culture could reframe American political thought. For him, the core question was always whether Africa was serviceable for the exploits of black American individualism, whether its natural resources were ripe for production, and whether its population could be moralized through Christianity.[42]

Even still, never was Delany's goal of emigration about justifying economic exploitation or political degradation. He refused to partake in the Western European Enlightenment's utopian trope of sanctified otherness—whether Jean-Jacques Rousseau's idea of the "noble savage" in *The Second Discourse* (1755) or Denis Diderot's fictional meditations on Tahitians in his *Supplement* (1772). Unlike the French philosophes, Delany approached human difference with the presumption of equality and complexity rather than flattening it to provide a romantic counterpoint to redeem and revitalize Western civilization. He described the Liberians he encountered as thoughtful and shrewd, intelligent and industrious. And he marveled at their market organization, sophisticated agricultural production techniques, and functional architecture.

UNREALIZED ESCAPE

Delany's utopian reflections were often contradictory, stifled by realism as much as brimming with unrealized idealism. He cultivated an image of moral clarity and political conviction in his emigrationism. But it was precisely in moments of vulnerability that his intellectual honesty exceeded his commitments. Delany's own life as something of a Renaissance figure—he was a physician, journalist, major, political propagandist and theorist, anthropologist, and novelist—embodied his defense of elite political rule. But it also revealed a figure who might have found unexpected common ground with the utopian socialists and feminists with which he would never be identified. Delany found equality, dignity, and freedom in black lives. He said no to white supremacy, exposed the drama of political contingency, and told of power's vulnerability. This was the vision Delany modeled to inspire resistance to reach black utopia abroad. But it wasn't extended to a defense of gender equality, popular rule, and economic freedom. This likely stemmed from Delany's unwillingness to dispense with American political convictions that he, like many Americans of his time, sincerely believed.

Ironically, had Delany followed through on the most radical democratic impulse of his utopian vision, he would have understood the meaning behind black feminist Anna Julia Cooper's critique of him in *A Voice from the South* (1892) as an "unadulterated black man" and her assertion that "no man can represent the race."[43] Even if he didn't accept the implications of his own vision, Delany nonetheless provided the very architecture for how to articulate a radical black imagination beyond the possible and to defend black utopia.

2

TURN-OF-THE-CENTURY BLACK LITERARY UTOPIANISM

Delany's death in 1885 came just before the rise of Jim Crow racial segregation in the 1890s. But this so-called nadir of black freedom dreams at the turn of the century did not evacuate the space for black utopianism. To the contrary, it generated what still remains the golden age of black utopian literature, which vividly developed the transformative vision of black citizenship Delany only outlined. Novelists such as Sutton E. Griggs (1872–1933), Frances Harper (1825–1911), Pauline E. Hopkins (1859–1930), and Edward A. Johnson (1860–1944) penned popular texts—pulp fiction, melodrama, and romance—for a political purpose. They moved black utopia from resistance to politics, from protest to world building, from critique centered upon white supremacy to utopia itself. All were public intellectuals that imagined a black future beyond the historical moment. They countered with a vision of equality and justice the racial segregation that became legal. They defended black dignity in the face of lynch mobs. Black utopian novelists were part of the cultural milieu that defined post-Emancipation black politics in terms of racial uplift. But their work rejected the racial accommodationism of the so-called Wizard of Tuskegee, the black educator Booker T. Washington, who urged black self-reliance over political agitation. They made applicable to black citizens the progressive vision of social reform circulating globally.

They offered an alternative to what was the best-selling and arguably most impactful literary work of their time: Edward Bellamy's utopian novel *Looking Backward* (1888), in which a white protagonist, Julian West, travels one hundred years into the future, in which the United States has become socialist.[1] Their version of black utopia was much democratic than Delany's. They added their voice to a growing chorus of American resistance to Gilded Age inequality. This is because they defended popular authority—where citizens were given the capacity to rule. Utopia, in their texts, was also much more critical, and elaborative of the complexities that Delany's work often avoided, if not consciously obscured. Political rule and community were explicitly connected to black freedom. Masculinity was exposed as exclusionary. And gender liberation was staunchly defended.

Griggs was a late-nineteenth-century African American Baptist minister who insisted upon strategic compromises between black citizens and white elites. But his *Imperium in Imperio* (1899), or "empire within an empire," whose title was drawn from a passage of *Looking Backward*, espoused a radical vision of pragmatic black self-rule. It did this through fictionalizing the inner workings of a secret shadow all-black republic operating in underground in Waco, Texas, to plot the overthrow of the Texas government.[2] Frances Harper was a prominent black progressive and first-wave feminist. Her novel *Iola Leroy* (1892), published seven years earlier, told the story of a light-skinned free black woman of aristocratic upbringing realizing her unknown black identity and becoming captured into slavery to envision a critical black public sphere.[3] Pauline Hopkins was a prolific black novelist whose commitment to political literature was realized through her involvement with one of the most widely read black journals of the time, *The Colored American Magazine*.[4] Her last serialized novel, *Of One Blood: or The Hidden Self* (1903), which imagined a hidden black civilization in Africa, set the stage for a future in which racism was abandoned and black culture was revered. Edward A. Johnson eventually became an elected member of the New York State Assembly in 1917, but his forgotten novel, *Light Ahead for the Negro*, used the genre of time travel to develop a utopian vision of economic equality. Many of these texts were ignored in the cultural mainstream, but their intended audience was black citizens. A nascent political theory about an ideal black future was embedded in their attempt to disrupt conventional wisdom about black society.

COMMUNITY AND RULE

Political community in black utopian literature textured what Delany's *The Condition* only outlined. Black self-government was freed from the constraints of white American racism and the imperatives of American national politics.[5] All four texts challenged Delany's defense of Platonic black elite rule. *Imperium*'s concluding dialogue in the Imperium's secret black congress dramatized competing ancient Greek utopian visions. The Spartan vision of authoritarian militaristic rule, exemplified by Bernard Belgrave, who defended race war, was juxtaposed against the Athenian one of civic patriotism. This was exemplified by Belton Piedmont's deference to the rule of law. But *Imperium*'s illustration of the tension between violence and nonviolence was less significant than its unifying vision of black politics. This combined democratic critique with republicanism in which elected leaders expressed their reasoned political judgments

FIGURE 2.1 Frances E. W. Harper

about black freedom. Though there is serious disagreement, there is also critical respect, push back, and evolving politics. But unlike the classic images of deliberation seen as exemplary in the American tradition during the Constitutional Convention of 1787—focused specifically on constitutional structures or political goods—*Imperium* defended politics as a matter of engaging with hierarchical power and social domination. It took seriously the idea of total liberation rather than narrowing its focus upon political rights.[6]

The conclusion of *Iola Leroy*, however, shifted utopia into the realm of the civic sphere. Through a fictitious debate between black citizens discussing concerns of black society—the role of women, the debate between immigration and assimilation, the necessity of religion, tolerance, civil rights, and education—*Iola Leroy* constructed its own Enlightenment public sphere. This privileged nonviolent deliberation about the public good over the necessity of political leadership.[7] Much of the concluding dialogue between Bishop Tunster (an emigrationist), Iola Leroy (a feminist), Professor Gradnor (a staunch patriot), and Miss Delany (a religious republican) is articulated through a set of probing questions rather than dogmatic answers, justification and elaboration rather than unquestioned assertion. Miss Delany's sentiment captured this: "I would have our people . . . more interested in politics. . . . We have never had a country with tender, precious memories. . . . We have been aliens and outcasts in the land of our birth. But I want my pupils to do all in their power to make this country worthy of their deepest devotion and loftiest patriotism."[8]

Without question, Harper's utopian counterpublic was both more self-critical than Griggs's and less accommodationist than Booker T. Washington's. It was also less masculine and more horizontal in its notion of power than both. But Griggs's anti-utopian critique of American culture's liberal promise was even more powerful than Harper's. *Imperium* directly implicated, rather than excused, American political thought in the perpetuation of violence and domination. Griggs's disenchantment with post-Emancipation American politics—the unchecked rise of lynching alongside the Republican Party's betrayal of the promise of Reconstruction—was fictionalized through way Belton is convicted of killing Dr. Zackland, a eugenicist who sees in him a perfect specimen to be analyzed and dissected, and who leads a mob to lynch him. Ironically, Belton is only exonerated in the Supreme Court with Bernard's defense. And Bernard himself only attains power as a US Democratic congressman in a Republican district through the ballot stuffing and fraud that he publicly rejects. Bernard declares what *Imperium*, following *The Condition*, insisted: the rule of law not only is manipulated by power, but justifies the power of the ruling class, which professes fidelity to it: "Before a court that has been lifted into power by the very hands of prejudice, justice need not be expected. The creature will, presumably, serve its creator; this much the creator demands."[9]

Imperium and *Iola Leroy* together imagined a postracist black politics freed from the fetters of white normative judgments. But neither fully elaborated or defended a future of interracial equality. This was the greatest achievement of Johnson's *Light Ahead for the Negro*. Whereas Griggs embraced his moment's political nationalism and Harper its cultural nationalism, Johnson embraced its social-democratic populism. *Light Ahead* was the first text to conceptualize the utopia of interracial freedom and egalitarian cooperation. And it moved black utopianism away from a focus upon elite leadership to direct popular rule, from a conversation about the moral integrity of masses to a defense of their intrinsic capacity for rule.[10]

Of the four texts, *Light Ahead* was by far the least dramatic and only rivaled *Imperium* in its use of didactic monologue to the reader. But what it lacked in terms of narrative complexity it gained in the clarity of its radical vision. Its protagonist, Gilbert Twitchell, who time-travels one hundred years into the future where the South is no longer racially authoritarian, sees technocratic organization fused with a direct democratic society. Popular referendum is the primary tool of decision-making and political elites are deposed. Ahead of its time was Johnson's defense of the viability of anarchism: *Light Ahead* imagined a polity without a president, Congress, or political appointees, and where economic freedom, worker's rights, complete political suffrage, and universal education were realized. The novel thus forcefully rejected myths of natural racial antipathy that eroded labor union and working-class solidarity.

The clearest antithesis to Johnson's political vision, however, was Hopkins's *Of One Blood*. By telling of the discovery of a glorious ancient Ethiopian Kingdom called "Tessalar," which is ruled by a queen, and comprises a council of twenty-five "Sages," appointed for life, *Of One Blood* valorized monarchy. But by presenting liberation as undertaken by black citizens themselves, *Of One Blood* rejected black inferiority. Ruel Briggs, a former Harvard black medical student, the novel's protagonist, is transformed from a denigrated black American passing as white in the United States into one of Tesslar's black leaders. He is not unlike Bernard, who is changed from detached black elite and beneficiary of the elected class to its greatest revolutionary enemy; Iola Leroy, who is changed from white aristocrat to black feminist; or Twitchell, who changes his posture from realism to idealism.

GENDER, FREEDOM, AND INDIVIDUALISM

Turn-of-the-century black utopian literature politicized gender.[11] Harper and Hopkins were activists for women's rights. They refused the presumption of unquestioned masculine authority evident in Delany. Ironically, although *Imperium* detailed the violence of intersectional domination for black women that *Iola Leroy* exposed—through discrimination in employment, denigration of epistemic authority, subjugation through marriage—Griggs refused to see it as problematic. Belton is demeaned by a white carriage driver who refuses to trust him to pay his fare at a later day and threatens his chivalry by asking payment from the woman he is with. Later in the novel, after being unable to get a job to support his family, he dons a wig to present himself as a black woman to get employment as a nurse. And after extended sexual harassment, which culminates in a plot to abduct and rape him by white men, he quits. The narrator writes, "He thought that while he was a nurse, he would do what he could to exalt the character of women . . . [but he] soon got the name of being a virtuous 'prude' and the white men decided to corrupt him at all hazards."[12]

Griggs's anxiety about emasculation was transformed into a vision of women's liberation in the novels of Hopkins and Harper. Both texts were limited by the ideology of first-wave feminism, which defended marriage, presumed a division of gendered labor, and valued the idea of civilized womanhood centered on etiquette and decorum. Indeed, *Of One Blood* stressed women's political rule through a matrilineal society and the queen of Tessalar. And *Iola Leroy* related black women's intersectional concerns in narrow relation to family life, while sometimes presenting women's freedom through moral purity and physical beauty. Nonetheless, unlike *Imperium*, these texts—along with *Light Ahead*—endowed women with political agency as leaders of social-service community organizations responsible for black uplift. Women were freed from the demands of unpaid domestic labor and envisioned not only as equal members in the skilled workforce but as intellectuals. This representation reversed the traditional split between public and private. It politicized the category of care work and motherhood.

Although none of the four texts escaped the appeal to respectability common in the post-Reconstruction-era literature of Paul Lawrence Dunbar, Charles Chestnutt, and James Weldon Johnson, all agreed that white supremacist reasoning would threaten a postracist future.[13] The most glaring example of this was in *Imperium*. Belton's theory of democratic loyalty contained a reactionary vision that deferred to the status quo. Griggs linked American historical amnesia found in Gilded Age individualism to the solidification of white supremacy. Belton, like Iola Leroy (who, before discovering her black blood, assumes herself to be a white southerner and is a defender of the slaveholder class), extended classic slaveholder reasoning. This had a long history in antebellum figures like John C. Calhoun and George Fitzhugh, but became updated in post-Reconstruction fiction, like Thomas Dixon's *The Leopard's Spots* (1902). Indeed, Belton depoliticizes history, recasts domination as a product of tradition, and justifies racial domination as a necessary price of Christian enlightenment.[14] Nowhere was this clearer than in his final speech:

> It was indeed an awful sin for the Anglo-Saxon to enslave the Negro. But in judging a people we must judge them according to the age in which they lived, and the influence that surrounded them. . . . When slavery was introduced into America, it was the universal practice of mankind to enslave. Knowing how quick we all are to heed the universal voice of mankind, we should be lenient toward others who are thus tempted and fall.[15]

Belton's conservative political theory was precisely what black literary utopianism warned against. He uses the idea of universal human fragility to justify compassion for hierarchical domination. In a striking reversal of power, he argues that increased compassion is necessary from the oppressed toward their oppressors. In this way, by transforming the historical experience of racist subjugation into a universal experience, he renders injustice immune from moral or political critique.

Black utopian literature warned that black self-governance would be undermined if white paternalistic authority were retained through citizens internalizing paternalistic ideas. For instance, Belton's white benefactor, V. M. King, teaches about the virtue of Christian pacifism and interracial love, while embracing myths of black intellectual inferiority. "A liberty-loving negro," he explained, was white people's "legitimate off-spring and not a bastard. . . . [But] the negro should not be over-boastful, and should recognize that the lofty conception of dignity of man and value and true character of liberty were taught to him by the Anglo-Saxon."[16] Dr. Gresham in *Iola Leroy* is a Northern abolitionist wanting to marry Iola, but is convinced of black political inferiority and white male superiority. Indeed, black utopian literature understood that strategic calculations to maintain existing status trumped moral virtues and political rationality lay hidden beneath public spectacles of good deeds. Securing and solidifying the longevity of white majority power, securing its rifts and fissures, is more important than ending white supremacy. This idea was forcefully echoed by Bernard, who suggests that Lincoln's Emancipation Proclamation of 1863 "came not so much as a message of love for the slave as a message of love for the Union."[17]

No less important for literary black utopianism was deconstructing white supremacist definitions of racial identity. The novels rejected white supremacist naturalizations of racism. These were popularized through post–Civil War Social Darwinist arguments about the "survival of the fittest" and by biologists like Francis Galton, who in 1865 coined the term *eugenics* and insisted upon "improving" the "breed" of humanity. In contrast, black utopians showed how black people were made, rather than were born, illiterate because they didn't receive minimally decent educations, and if they did, it was only to secure the rule of elite authority and its standards of rectitude: "they give us fewer and inferior school building," Barnard says, "they attempt to muzzle the mouths of negro teachers, and he who proclaims too loudly the doctrine of equality as taught by Thomas Jefferson, will soon be in search of other employment."[18] Likewise, black citizens become viewed as "unclean" not because of personal moral deficiency but because they are arbitrarily forced into the most physically taxing and lethal work the white majority won't do.[19]

This is why a central objective of literary black utopianism was the presumption of black freedom. This was assumed as a premodern Afro-reality in *Of One Blood*, in which universal equality existed beyond the confines of the Euro-modern experience. *Light Ahead* imagined it as part of modernity's overcoming of social, class, and gender inequities in the form of future interracial equality. But to retell the future differently it was also necessary to retell the past. For this reason, *Imperium* represented racial domination based on chains, not neighborly greetings, lashes, not proclamations of liberty, tearing of flesh, not nourishment. As Bernard says:

> When in 1619 our forefathers landed on the American shore, the music of welcome with which they were greeted, was the clanking of iron chains ready to fetter them; the crack of the whip to be used to plow furrows in their backs; and the yelp of the bloodhound who was to bury his fangs deep into their flesh, in case they sought for liberty. Such was the music with which the Anglo-Saxon came down to the shore to extend a hearty welcome to the forlorn children of night, brought from a benighted heathen land to a community of *Christians.*[20]

Imperium disrupted consensus narratives of US history that stressed abstract universal ideals. Such principles gave off the patina of realism, helping to distract from and create intellectual distance from principled acts of domination. Their universalism—these principles claimed to serve as a check or uncompromising witness against atrocity—masked the terror of everyday life. Liberty is proclaimed as the end of American virtue, but *Imperium*'s black citizen sees that America is decidedly unethical. *Imperium* thus paralleled *Iola Leroy*'s retelling of the re-enslavement of freed black citizens, which modeled futuristic citizenship mindful of historical context, the constraints of social structure, and the limitation of unfettered free will.

Imperium was the clearest rejection of American individualism, but the other three texts reimagined its meaning. *Of One Blood* revised it as a sense of adventure, self-examination, and personal growth through Briggs's journey. And *Iola Leroy*'s long dialogues about the ethics of slavery, the causes of the Civil War, the meaning of gender liberation, the possibility of interracial cooperation, and white paternalism not only fashioned individualism as a matter of liberal pluralistic expression. It also extended it to racial equality—where different accounts of the good and political strategy were debated nonviolently. *Light Ahead* redefined individualism as individuality in the iconoclastic way of pushing hierarchical boundaries on social arrangements and conventions. Johnson embraced Nietzsche's idea of artistic self-invention and humanistic faith in freedom—as Twitchell puts it, "Individuality gives room for thought, out of which is born invention and progress."[21]

The wreckage of the Gilded Age, which produced massive levels of economic inequality through "robber barons" like Rockefeller, Carnegie, and Vanderbilt, provided the context for black utopian literature to theorize the future of capitalism.[22] *Iola Leroy* paid little attention to the problem of economic inequality, but revised the racial boundaries of the American dream by inserting the black bourgeoisie as its legitimate heirs in ways unacceptable to the Jim Crow lynch mobs that murdered black business owners throughout the South. And like *Light Ahead*, it also stressed the economic dimensions of enslavement. More so than the other texts, *Of One Blood* glorified capitalism through

Briggs's awe at the gold, diamonds, jewelry, and monuments of Tessalar and his striking disregard for the degrading conditions through which they were produced. *Imperium* never defended socialism or communism, but its representation of Bernard's philosophy expressed a progressive vision that understood the way capitalism deprived people of good choices and made their bodies into profit-making machines. As Bernard says, "The negro was seized and forced to labor hard that the Anglo-Saxon might enjoy rest and ease. While he sat in his cushioned chair, in his luxurious home, and dreamed of the blessedness of freedom, the enforced labor of slaves . . . receiv[ed] therefor no manner of pay, no token of gratitude, no word of coldest thanks."[23] *Imperium* opposed accounts of domination that deemphasized its formative role for white wealth. Necessary too was it for black citizens to think in terms of corrective collective responsibility—redistributive compensation or reparations for past injustice. This nascent idea of socioeconomic distribution in *Imperium* was clearly developed in *Light Ahead*. Johnson realized the dream of socialists in painting a picture in which predominately white labor unions would organize across the racial line for better pay, shorter hours, and more adequate working conditions. In Johnson's socialist utopia, no longer were strikes or lockouts prevalent because the "the chief concern of the labor unions now is to raise their less skillful members to a higher standard."[24]

IDENTITY AND HUMANITY BEYOND RACISM

Racial solidarity became a central concern, even if a contested question, of black literary utopianism. *Imperium* denounced racialist thinking. Bernard's social privilege can't prevent his black wife, Viola, from committing suicide, because, internalizing US antimiscegenation ideology that Delany himself embraced in the 1880s, she believes her relationship with him, a multiracial man, only dilutes the purity of the black race and threatens its extinction and she tells him to commit his life to racial separatism.[25] *Light Ahead* replaced *Imperium*'s vision of race-consciousness with class-consciousness, which trumped firm ideological commitments to nationhood, gender, and culture. And *Of One Blood* shared *Iola Leroy*'s ideal of racial impurity that unsettled expectations about the meaning of belonging. Nonetheless, all four novels shared the core revelation around which *Of One Blood* was structured. As the narrator asks, "but who is clear enough in vision to decide who hath black blood and who hath it not? Can any one tell? . . . no man can draw the dividing line between the two races, for they are both of one blood!"[26] Moreover, Belton's concluding words, that the pen is "mightier" than the sword, constituted what was both *Imperium*'s and black literary utopianism's defense of pragmatic political community formation through argument, law, and claim-making. As Belton says, "If denied the use of the ballot let us devote our attention to that mightier weapon, the pen."[27] Behind this argument for racial uplift was a defense of improvised black political possibility, which could take action in unexpected directions.

Indeed, future black citizenship in *Imperium* was based on neither violence nor nonviolence, but upon emergent political conditions. As Belton put it, politics "courts a peaceable adjustment, yet it does not shirk war, if war is forced."[28] Likewise, *Iola Leroy*'s concluding image of a black civil sphere was pluralistic. Iola is a caregiving nurse and feminist, Dr. Latimer, her black husband, is both a physician and a defender of global human rights, and their friends are seen organizing successful schools and civic centers. *Of One Blood*'s conclusion with Briggs fleeing America to assume his throne in Africa redrew the boundaries of black political commitment and community beyond the nation-state, while *Light Ahead*'s vision of black politics combined elements of socialism and liberalism.

The political limitations of black literary utopianism problematize its utility today. But it cannot stifle its intellectual and cultural radicalism. This work's investment in patriotism echoed hegemonic narratives that were mobilized to engage in American imperialist adventures in the Philippines, Cuba, Hawaii, Panama, Haiti, Mexico, and Nicaragua. But this work deconstructed naïve progressivism that focused on colorblind class solutions to inequality but avoided white supremacy. It rejected individualism narrowly focused upon economic prosperity divorced from collective responsibility. It dismantled Social Darwinist myths of natural inferiority and superiority that justified Jim Crow and lynching. Most significantly, black figures who were given no license for freedom in American discourse were reimagined as crucial for its perpetuation. Democratic possibility that was burgeoning in the progressive moment was given a new lease on life.

3

W. E. B. DU BOIS'S WORLD OF UTOPIAN INTIMACY

Black utopianism would be elaborated in a figure with whom it was rarely associated, but who was the towering black intellectual of the twentieth century: W. E. B Du Bois (1868–1963). Du Bois is best remembered for his black progressivism in the founding of the NAACP (National Association for Colored People) in 1909 and its publication, *The Crisis*, which focused on political enfranchisement, labor rights, and antilynching legislation. But Du Bois was so much more. His evolving and contradictory intellectual commitments over his ninety-five years expressed the vacillating mood of black political thought. He was, at first, an American patriot who thought American institutions provided a remedy for racial injustice, before becoming an avowed Pan-Africanist socialist. A diligent social scientist who complied data to expose black socioeconomic inequality before becoming a radical Marxist who saw capitalism as central in perpetuating racial domination. A progressive before he was a communist. A peace activist before he was a eulogizer of a totalitarian, Joseph Stalin of the Soviet Union, and later Kwame Nkrumah in Ghana (despite his increasing authoritarian tendencies), where he died in 1963.[1]

Du Bois's politics was shifting and complex, but was always suffused with a spirit of idealism. And in the 1920s this was

FIGURE 3.1 W. E. B. Du Bois

especially clear in his fiction. The ruptures and dislocations created by the end of the Great War, the emergent ethnic nationalisms, the Bolshevik Revolution of 1917, progressivism, and the suffragette struggle presented Du Bois a unique opportunity to think about humanity's future. Though they have long been ignored as rich political theoretical texts, his short story "The Comet" (1920) as part of his text *Darkwater* (1920) and his novel

Dark Princess (1928) painted an image of utopian possibility where people of color had autonomy of their lives. "The Comet" describes utopia as an experience of postracist interracial existence after a comet has destroyed New York City, while *Dark Princess* imagined it as a Global South movement for decolonized political rule. Du Bois's utopias were multiple, but nonetheless shared a countercultural philosophical and ethical vision of American culture. Not only in their unabashed faith in hope, but in their willingness to challenge core suppositions about identity, community, and recognition.[2] Unlike his utopian predecessors, Du Bois both expanded the tradition to more explicitly include interracial democracy and Afro-Asian solidarity and introduced a self-consciously critical understanding of utopia.[3]

RECONSTRUCTING HOPE FROM THE ASHES

"The Comet" was Du Bois's meditation on the contours of an impossible future to be erected upon the rubble of a collapsed institutionalized hierarchy. The widespread destruction—as Jim, a black messenger, and Julia, a white wealthy housewife, scour the streets for survivors from the comet's wreckage—was as much a metaphor for human finitude as it was a beginning for an emancipatory interracial ethics not governed by domination. The deafening silence that pervades New York's streets was as much Du Bois's reflection on the fragility of social life as it was an opportunity for him to imagine communication unfettered by social convention. And the crumbled skyscrapers dotting the landscape became an opportunity for Du Bois to explore the towering inequities of capitalism as well as to imagine new communal formulations not driven by exploitation.

By presenting an ideal interracial moment of intimacy briefly consummated between Jim and Julia, Du Bois imagined what seemed impossible throughout much of US history:

> They stared a moment in silence. She had not noticed before that he was a Negro. He had not thought of her as white. She was a woman of perhaps twenty-five—rarely beautiful and richly gowned, with darkly-golden hair, and jewels. Yesterday, he thought with bitterness, she would scarcely have looked at him twice. He would have been dirt beneath her silken feet. She stared at him. Of all the sorts of men she had pictured as coming to her rescue she had not dreamed of one like him. Not that he was not human, but he dwelt in a world so far from hers, so infinitely far, that he seldom even entered her thought. Yet as she looked at him curiously he seemed quite commonplace and usual. He was a tall, dark workingman of the better class, with a sensitive face trained to stolidity and a poor man's clothes and hands. His face was soft and slow and his manner at once cold and nervous, like fires long banked, but not out.[4]

Critics would accuse Du Bois of never wavering from his racial essentialism, which attributed a spiritual and hereditary quality to racial identity. But "The Comet" was part of Du Bois's wish to make deconstruction constructive, to transform the loss of identity into a new knowledge, in the service of his lifelong project of dismantling white supremacy.[5] By stressing new recognitions and collapsed distinctions, new identities being born from "silence" and through a sense of intellectual disorientation, which appears "commonplace and usual" in the newfound rupture,[6] Du Bois switched the focus from what had been his most famous text, *The Souls of Black Folk* (1903). *Souls*'s articulation of what Du Bois thought was an undiscovered black identity, of a double consciousness, of being both black and American, became in "The Comet" a vision of an unknown postracist community, which expressed racism's epistemological disorientation and humanity's reconstruction.[7] In contrast to progressive reformers of the moment like Jane Addams, Herbert Croly, and Upton Sinclair who turned their sympathetic gaze outward to assist impoverished citizens, Du Bois challenged the value of recognition itself. Failure of recognition, rather than its achievement, became emancipatory. Gone was the certainty of affixing definitive value to skin-color when Julia, first, forgets race—she doesn't see Jim as "black"—and, then, after she remembers it, doubts the moral weight she places on it. Du Bois thus dismantled knowledge based on utopian scientific rationality, that everything could be measured, known, tested, fully understood. Value instead came from the failure to fully recognize social meaning and, instead, a sensitivity to human expressiveness—the different gestures, tones of voice, and textures of speech—that provides cues for responding to and engaging with the person who appears before them. "The Comet" presented this moment beyond reason or reasonableness. It escaped categorization, of mapping one's identity into a larger scheme of social understanding, which contained all of its crystallized misperceptions and misapprehensions.

This is why Du Bois's postracist ethics in "The Comet" was more influenced by St. Augustine's notion of tragic humanity—in which loss, failure, and vulnerability were inescapable parts of life in the "City of Man"—than a teleological vision of increasing rationalization.[8] "The Comet" was thus the first black utopian text that prioritized shared precariousness over natural rights or historical genealogies of universal humanity in the service of achieving racial liberation—"The rich and the poor are met together," Jim and Julia agree, "how foolish our human distinctions seem—now."[9]

Connected to this was Du Bois's upending of the meaning of community. It became unformed and fluid, organized less around rational communication and realized objectives and more around the shared presence in the face of the unknown. As the narrator puts it, "then the thought of the dead world without rushed in and they started toward each other."[10] Du Bois rendered their intimacy speechless—as not confined by words, of a togetherness based in shared solitude, as a struggle to articulate rather than easily realize wants, communicate feelings, and listen.[11] Here Du Bois centralized the obligation to respond in ways that anticipated what the French postwar philosopher Emmanuel Levinas would later call a "face-to-face" ethics.[12] Du Bois broadened this Levinasian idea of interpersonal responsibility collectively. By describing how Jim and Julia look for their respective families and any other survivors—first moving along the streets of New York's affluent, white midtown neighborhood before going to its predominately working-class black one in Harlem—Du Bois transformed responsibility from something that depended upon realizing fixed moral objectives to something that dealt with addressing immediate problems at hand. As Du Bois wrote,

> Yet as the two, flying and alone, looked upon the horror of the world, slowly, gradually, the sense of all-enveloping death deserted them. They seemed to move in a world silent and asleep,—not dead. They moved in quiet reverence, lest somehow they wake these sleeping forms who had, at last, found peace. . . . To both, the vision of a mighty beauty—of vast, unspoken things, swelled in their souls.[13]

Fixed community is not a precondition for politics; it is a work in progress to be realized. Utopia requires struggle because a politics based on shared vulnerability is hard. Communicating and acting need to be reimagined not as solutions to problems, but as problems to be worked through and worked on, to be deconstructed and reconstructed.

But Du Bois unsettled expectations as quickly as he reimagined them. He was too perceptive in his dialectical analysis of racism to naïvely insist upon the romantic resolutions of what American culture embraced wholesale. In swift narrative disorientation, Du Bois subverted postracist solidarity precisely by what made it possible. Loneliness came from collapsed community. Anxiety came from finitude. Du Bois's astute knowledge of the cyclical nature of American history—from the rise of the KKK (Ku Klux Klan) during Reconstruction, to its abandonment by Republican antiracist allies and the virtual silence on race by progressive friends who claimed to be political allies—made him aware of the malleability of white supremacy and fragility of black freedom. What appeared so transformative became derailed by what was so familiar. As the narrative unfolds, Julia begins to see Jim as "an alien in blood and culture—unknown, perhaps unknowable," and wishes to escape him as quickly as possible. Here Du Bois dramatized the dark side of vulnerability. He believed whiteness was intoxicating, masking the human fragility, fear, insecurity, confusion, and ambiguity beneath it.[14] An unknowable future of postwhiteness became too terrifying for white citizens and so an unrealized community became completed through the return of fixed identities. Not knowing where communication might go, what paths freedom might take, and what kind of unsanctioned feelings it might generate facilitated withdrawal, rather than greater solidarity.[15]

Though his own household was deeply patriarchal and, as commentators have claimed, *Souls* implicitly connected political rule to masculinity,[16] one of the greatest dangers to utopia in "The

Comet" is gender hierarchy. Denouncing gender hierarchy as threatening to utopia stemmed from Du Bois's philosophical commitment to feminism. Du Bois insisted that "the future woman" was to have freedom in the workplace and within the family, economic independence, and full education.[17] By describing Julia's admiration of Jim as a chivalrous gentleman, defined by a glorified, "vigorous manhood,"[18] Du Bois prophesized that making masculinity redemptive of blackness would leave intact the narrative of aggressive black male sexuality perpetuated by turn-of-the-century lynch mobs murdering black men. Indeed, what Julia fails to reimagine is what the symbolic standard bearer of American culture, the white racist man and her partner, Fred, holds as utter faith. Unuttered words and unannounced futures of postracist possibility are snatched from them when, in the conclusion, Fred, who, along with Julia's father, is alive and well, asks first whether she has been raped by Jim, who he calls a "nigger"—which is what a gathering white crowd calls him, before threatening to lynch him.

The unspoken word, the silence, the lack of rational communication, which Du Bois described earlier in the story as a space of liberation, is ultimately seized by power. Postracism evaporates when history resurfaces, accompanied by its lethal fantasies of violence, its pervasive disrespect, its inflexible identities and white innocence. Du Bois thus undercut teleological views of the triumph of racial justice by connecting Julia's latent racist paternalism with Julia's father, who tells Jim that he always liked his "people" and proceeds to offer him a job. At the same time, Jim's concluding embrace of his black wife—who also is unexpectedly alive, though their child isn't—allowed Du Bois not only to invert white racist myths of the absence of black love but also to lay bare the pragmatic underpinnings of black nationalism that were burgeoning in New York during the 1920s with the rise of Marcus Garvey and his UNIA (Universal Negro Improvement Association).[19]

NEW WORLDS, GLOBAL VISIONS

A decade after writing "The Comet," in *Dark Princess* Du Bois shifted his literary utopianism from US interracial postracism to his lifelong support of global antiracist political solidarity among nonwhite people.[20] *Dark Princess* chronicled the relationship between Matthew Townes, a black American, and Princess Kautilya of Bwodpur, a member of the Indian royal family, who is the principal architect of a secretive committee of the Great Council of the Darker Races planning global emancipation for people of color. The novel's structure as a romance was meant for popular consumption, but expressed a powerful meditation on democratic possibility.

Dark Princess's sustained critique of antiegalitarian orderings of identity challenged what critics perceived as Du Bois's own political elitism, aristocratic tastes, and problematic moralizing of the black masses that often resembled that of his intellectual foe, Booker T. Washington. *Dark Princess*'s overarching argument is that internalizing narratives of successful political development stifled the possibility of political action. This is captured through one of the Council's Japanese representatives, who tells Townes upon their first meeting in Berlin that black Americans are "cowards," who are lagging behind culturally.[21] *Dark Princess*'s objection to such absolutist hierarchical thinking is detailed in the formative debate between Townes and Perigua—a black nationalist leader modeled on Garvey. Perigua tells Townes "your caution is ignorance inbred for ten generations."[22] For Du Bois, equating political critique with unmanliness and using violence to bolster it silenced counterarguments necessary for freedom. Indeed, Townes's inability to organize a successful labor strike of Chicago Pullman Porters doesn't illuminate greater understanding of his intersectional oppression as a working-class black man. Instead, it leads him to withdraw from transformative action. "I had thought once that I might help," Townes tells Kautilya after he is imprisoned after his eventual involvement in Perigua's thwarted attack on Klansmen who had lynched his black friend, "That dream is gone. I made a mistake, and now I can only help by bowing beneath the yoke of shame; and by that very deed I am hindered—forever—to help you—or any one—much."[23]

Dark Princess was suspicious of unreconstructed patriarchy. This is displayed through Townes's denigration of the political acumen of Sara Andrews—a black bourgeois woman, and secretary to African American political boss Sammy Scott, who facilitates his release from prison—as nothing more than self-interested manipulation and through his attraction to her appearance because she is pure, prim, and saint-like. The narrator describes Sara as having "no particular scruples or conscience. Lying, stealing, bribery, gambling, prostitution were facts that she accepted casually. . . . [She was] personally honest and physically 'pure' almost to prudery."[24]

As a consequence of Du Bois's increasing orientation toward Marxism in 1920s, *Dark Princess* denounced American capitalist individualism and elite power that earlier black utopians embraced. Townes ruthlessly moves up the political ranks with Sara and Sammy's help as he goes through the Illinois state legislature before being on the verge of a nomination to US Congress. His initial philosophy of revolutionary anticolonialism devolves into a radical cynicism based on personal enrichment. As the narrator describes it, Townes "had no illusions as to American democracy. . . . He knew the power of organized crime, of self-indulgence, of industry, business, corporations, finance, commerce."[25] *Dark Princess* enacted the very civic republican critique of elite rule leveled against Du Bois and the NAACP: that their concern with social prominence, immersion in circles of power, and increasing financial prosperity took attention away from the interests of the black majority.

Dark Princess's conclusion answered the question that had long preoccupied Du Bois—Who should rule? Both its answer and unrealized vision paralleled the complex vision of earlier black utopian texts. While defending the enlightened vanguard that Du Bois personally supported, *Dark Princess* outlined an opposing justification for popular governance.[26] Townes's antidemocratic skepticism stemmed from Du Bois's worry about white supremacist populism, which was evident in everything from the nineteenth-century Anti-Federalist defense of states' rights and Jacksonian democracy to twentieth-century Jim Crow segregation. And Du Bois's own view resonated with the broader American cultural mood exemplified by one of his acquaintances, Walter Lippmann, whose *Public Opinion* (1922) claimed that popular ignorance threw democratic faith into question.[27]

But Du Bois countered Townes's defense of oligarchic rule with Kautilya's transformation from royal heir to working-class political actor. Kautilya first enacts self-defense against a white employer who tries to rape her, which empowers her to participate in a labor movement, and then a strike, for which she is beaten and eventually jailed. She, as a woman domestic worker, describes her act as a "lesson he needed" and, as a factory worker, is "aghast" at "labor of the lowest type."[28] Compared to Townes involvement with the Pullman Porters, Kautilya's immersion in the life of labor—as a domestic worker in Virginia and in factories in Pennsylvania and New York—leads to an enlarged theoretical vision, giving her greater awareness about the multilayered nature of intersectional domination based on class and gender. Kautilya's reconstituted image of working-class citizenship opposed Du Bois's justification for elite rule that turned on the idea that ordinary citizens were lacking sufficient political intelligence. She says, "that which began as a game and source of experience to me suddenly became life. I became an agent, organizer, and officer of the union. I knew my fellow laborers, in home and street."[29] Ordinary people organizing together and acting in ways to challenge their oppression without elite rule precisely because of their experience of domination is *Dark Princess*'s challenge to Townes's view that the masses are easily exploitable. In this sense, the novel felt less like it was indebted to Lippman and more to John Dewey, with whom Du Bois founded a short-lived League for Independent Action (LIPA) in 1929 to develop a third political party and whose faith in democracy came from his awareness that ordinary people developed knowledge of self-rule in local contexts.

Just as *Dark Princess* embraced elite political rule it also revised rule itself as a flexible critical activity. Here, positions are reimagined, deeply held convictions are undone, and certainties are dismantled. This is evident not only in Kautilya's transformation but in Townes's abandonment of the American dream of upward mobility for the struggle for a more just world. Kautilya's equation of democracy with oligarchy—"your oligarchy . . . it is democracy, if only the selection of oligarchs is just and true"[30]—expressed Du Bois's revision of "aristocracy." Aristocracy here is not found through birth or expressed through exceptional wealth or singular intellectual capacity, but is evident through countering exploitative reasoning and practices that the first two parts of the novel identified as endemic to American culture. "The mission of the darker people, my Kautilya, of black and brown and yellow," Townes says, embodying the realization of Du Bois's defense of social democracy, "is to raise out of their pain, slavery, and humiliation, a beacon to guide manhood to health and happiness and life and away from the morass of hate, poverty, crime, sickness, monopoly, and the mass-murder called war."[31]

UTOPIA IN THE RUBBLE OF DEMOCRACY

Darkwater and *Dark Princess* captured Du Bois's lifelong vacillation between pessimism and hope. On the one hand, Du Bois's skepticism about realizing postracist utopia was detailed through the tragic conclusion of "The Comet" and *Dark Princess*'s uncertain one with the birth of Townes and Kautilya's multiracial son, who the novel described as a vulnerable infant. On the other hand, *Dark Princess*'s description of this child as a "messiah," along with *Darkwater*'s concluding poem, which called for making "Humanity divine!," illustrated Du Bois's defense of human potential.[32] In both of these texts, the suffering, pain, violence, and marginalization associated with "darkness" are as apparent as the light—the reflection of beauty and resilience in the ocean of a reimagined blackness. Although Du Bois never defended direct participatory democracy, he defended the idea of social democracy, which he saw as an expansive and sacred ideal. As he put it in *Darkwater*'s essay, "Of the Ruling of Men," it was "a method of realizing the broadest measure of justice to all human beings."[33]

For Du Bois, democracy illuminated something of the dialectic between beginnings and ends, struggles and reversals, progress and reaction, change and uncertainty, the unknown and the unknown unknown.[34] For all these contradictions, it was the aspiration to live in a democracy that, Du Bois believed, could rebuild the world in which all Americans would want to live. This was where, as he said in his utopian call to arms in *Darkwater*'s opening "Credo," they could "stretch their arms and their souls, [have] the right to breathe and the right to vote, the freedom to choose their friends, enjoy the sunshine, and ride on the railroads, uncursed by color; thinking, dreaming, working as they will in a kingdom of beauty and love."[35] But if "The Comet" and *Dark Princess* were any indication, achieving this world required a utopian imagination that gave life to the unspoken, uncertain, and unknown, that found freedom in acknowledgment and revision, that saw beauty and authority in everyday struggle and experience. Maintaining this required probing analysis of its unseen betrayals.

Darkwater and *Dark Princess* were fictional statements about the fundamental interconnection between beauty and death on the American racial scene when the question of what to build in the rubble of global war was on everyone's minds. But its utopianism also came from the hope that citizens could be saved from their worst impulses, that they could live meaningfully, nonviolently in their everyday encounters and politics.

4

GEORGE S. SCHUYLER, IRONY, AND UTOPIA

Black utopian thought continued with one of the leading figures of the Harlem renaissance, the essayist and novelist George S. Schuyler (1895–1977). By the end of his life, Schuyler was best remembered for his postwar conservatism. His autobiography, *Black and Conservative* (1966), had scathing remarks about the civil rights movement and professed allegiance to anticommunist McCarthyism. Schuyler himself once had membership in the nativist Birch Society. All of this likely explains why, despite his status as one of the preeminent public intellectuals of his time, political theorists have been so reluctant to examine his insights.[1]

But in the 1930s—the moment when he was at his creative peak, Schuyler was a socialist, who was described as the black H. L. Mencken for his searing social commentary and cultural critique in what was then the most widely circulated black newspaper in the United States, the *Pittsburgh Courier.* At the time, nothing bothered Schuyler more than "true believers" who sacrificed complexity in favor of rigid ideology. This is what encouraged him to undertake a project that few did with such irreverence and humor: an influential literary engagement with utopia in two texts. *Black No More* (1931) treated a technological solution—a corrosive medical procedure that gave black people

FIGURE 4.1 George S. Schuyler. Library of Congress, Prints and Photographs Division, Carl Van Vechten Collection, LC-USZ62–95999.

white skin—as a false promise for racial liberation.[2] And his two stories "The Black Internationale" and "Black Empire" were published in serial form between 1936 and 1938 in the *Courier*, which would later be called *Black Empire*, under the pseudonym Samuel I. Brooks. They parodied the prospect of global black power through the story of an authoritarian black empire.

No doubt, Schuyler was the first prominent black antiutopian thinker. However, he was more like the ancient Greek satirist Aristophanes, who lampooned Athenian convictions in democracy and its intellectual culture, rather than Thrasymachus in Plato's *Republic*, whose skepticism of justice led to an embrace of the idea that "might makes right." Schuyler's satires in the vein of Jonathan Swift, Alexander Pope, and Voltaire were unlike anything in the utopian tradition. This is because they examined not his own vision, but the dominant ideas circulating within American society—the progressive dream of postracialism, of black assimilation into white culture, of an unproblematic racial passing, and Pan-Africanism. Despite this wide-ranging critique, however, Schuyler's work ultimately shared a crucial idea with the black utopian tradition. It insisted that the dream of postracism would be stillborn unless Americans deconstructed entrenched cultural ideologies.

POSTRACIAL FANTASIES, AMERICAN STYLE

Schuyler's skepticism about the redemptive possibilities of progressive American social science informed *Black No More*'s narrative. The novel rejected the idea of "Chicago School" sociologists, led by Robert E. Park and his students. Amid the waves of immigration to the United States in the early twentieth century, their "racial relations cycle" argued that racial assimilation into white Anglo-American values would be the eventual outcome for black Americans.[3] In contrast, *Black No More* objected to black assimilation precisely because of the dominant culture—American exploitative logics of patriarchy, capitalism, inequality, and instrumentalism. Though it was clearly a satire meant to provoke and scandalize, *Black No More* doubly earned the scorn of both American patriots and black racial uplift advocates. This is because it controversially suggested that only violence and false hope would come from the American equation of happiness with male honor and economic wealth. Or as the novel's black protagonist, Max Disher, puts it, "three things essential to the happiness of a colored gentleman" are "yellow money, yellow women and yellow taxis."[4] Nowhere was *Black No More*'s thesis clearer than in the novel's opening scene, where, after he is rebuffed at a dance club and called a "nigger" by a blond-haired, blue-eyed Southern woman, Disher fantasizes about reversing the ban on US antimiscegenation policy. This is conveyed in a dream in which he dines and dances with her, and is atop a golden throne before white slaves, just before a lynch mob arrives on the scene. He "dreamed of dancing with her, dining with her, motoring with her, sitting beside her on a golden throne while millions of manacled white slaves prostrated themselves before him. Then there was a nightmare of grim, gray men with shotguns, baying hounds, a heap of gasoline-soaked faggots and a screeching, fanatical mob."[5] *Black No More* retold as distinctly American, first, the possessiveness that white racists desired but had long projected upon an imagined hypersexuality of black men. And, second, the racial violence such projections had produced.[6]

Despite the novel's seemingly linear narrative trajectory from racial difference to universal whiteness, from racialism to postracialism when black skin is virtually eliminated, *Black No More* refused the idea of progress. Instead, it favored what Nietzsche, who Schuyler admired, called "eternal recurrence."[7] The novel ends where it begins. But Disher—who, after taking the Black-No-More procedure, becomes a spokesperson for the Knights of Nordica, a white supremacist organization modeled on the Ku Klux Klan—isn't the one lynched. Instead, it's the two intellectual white supremacists—Samuel Buggerie, a prominent eugenicist, and Arthur Snobbcraft, the Democratic nominee for vice president. This is because their genealogical research ironically reveals to the public that both of them, like the vast majority of white citizens, have black ancestry. Outrage ensues and both men try to flee. To avoid recognition, they don black shoe polish on their faces to pass as black to hide their identities. But, after their plane runs out of gas, they accidently arrive in Happy Hill, Mississippi, which is the home of rabid white supremacists who lynch them.

Happy Hill's ringleader, Rev. McPhule, who speaks of the lynching as his life's "crowning ambition" before taking a hundred dollar bill from Snobbcraft's pocket, is not unlike Fisher, whose acquisitive individualism leads him to disregard white supremacist terror and racism.[8] The concluding lynching scene suggests that both white supremacy and capitalist inequality are so difficult to renounce because they are affective rather than rational, invested in a libidinal pleasure economy of desire—of surplus, risk, excitement, and death. The narrator describes how Happy Hill residents "envisioned the passing of an old, established custom. Now there was nothing left to stimulate them but the old time religion and the clandestine sex orgies."[9] This is why the novel's epilogue prophesized the continuation of racial commodification in a postblack world. The black inventor of Black-No-More, Dr. Junius Crookman, now US surgeon general, publishes a book on the differences in pigmentation that says the so-called new Caucasians are physically lighter than the old ones, which are of a pinkish complexion. Consequently, these new Caucasians are segregated, are paid less, and form a Down-with-White-Prejudice-League. They do this while the upper classes find a way to get darker and adopt stained skin, which becomes fashionable—as "Everybody that was anybody had a stained skin."[10]

Central to *Black No More* was a deconstruction of American "rugged individualism," popularized by president Herbert

Hoover in the 1920s. Nowhere was Schuyler's critique of the commodification and mass consumption of the period so vividly captured than through the superficial feeling of liberation Fisher feels. Being "free" from the "tyranny" of his black nose and "nappy hair" and seeing his smooth, milky white hands make him feel like "an American citizen."[11] In this regard, *Black No More* was an existential critique of whiteness. Drawing an arresting parallel between the racist capitalist exploitation of black bodies and Fisher's exploitation of his whiteness, Schuyler rendered whiteness static. It was a narrow self-interested pursuit that bankrupted self-examination and political solidarity. Not only is Fisher "through with coons,"[12] but he becomes a leading white supremacist for the sake of personal enrichment. Fisher is not unlike the imperial grand wizard, Rev. Henry Givens, the leader of the Knights of Nordica, who exhibits and rationalizes the very criminal, conniving, duplicitous identity of which he presumptively accuses black people. Givens had been " a hard worker in withdrawing as much money from its treasury as possible," convincing himself that he wasn't stealing, but simply appropriating a "rightful reward for his valuable services."[13] His wife, Mrs. Givens, is no different. She "had the reputation among her friends of not always stating the exact truth; she hated Negroes . . . but she was a devout Christian no one doubted."[14] In Schuyler's telling, concealing lack of virtue requires reversing its meaning. Hard work becomes exploitation. Theft a natural right. Morality synonymous with denigration. *Black No More* was thus an account of how white supremacy represses and rationalizes this process. Whiteness becomes an organized religion. One submits to its fixed identity to wash away their contradictions. But there is a cost; it is morally deadening.

Schuyler fancied himself as an artist of the first order, an individualist associated with the figures that composed the Harlem

Renaissance—Alain Locke, James Weldon Johnson, Langston Hughes, and Zora Neale Hurston. But *Black No More* was nothing less than a searing indictment of its philosophy of racial uplift.[15] Schuyler was a booster of black business, but *Black No More*'s view was that black economic elites continued the racial inequality that originated with white slaveholders. This is visualized in a scene of armed riot police and a taut steel cable surrounding a queue of black people waiting to get skin-treatment in Crookman's Harlem sanitarium: "In front of the sanitarium milled a half-frozen crowd of close to four thousand Negroes. A riot squad armed with rifles, machine guns and tear gas bombs maintained some semblance of order. A steel cable stretched from lamp post to lamp post . . . [and] kept the struggling mass of humanity on the sidewalk. It seemed as if all Harlem were there."[16] Opposed here is an organic singular black community that earlier black utopians defended. Denounced here also are formulations of black politics unmoored from democratic accountability.

Indeed, the ire that Schuyler reserved for black elites like Du Bois and Garvey in his editorials at the *Courier* was unleashed in *Black No More* in the way it collapsed the ideological distinctions between integration and separatism. For instance, Dr. Shakespeare Agamemnon Beard, a black progressive social reformer, modeled on Du Bois, and his organization, National Social Equality League, a riff on the NAACP, is not unlike the black nationalist, Santop Licorice, modeled on Garvey. *Black No More* saw moral hypocrisy sustaining black elite rule. The NSEL eventually combines with other leaders with widely opposed interests to pragmatically urge the US attorney general to jail Crookman. And Licorice colludes with the Knights of Nordica. Black political solidarity to build a new polity becomes a zero-sum game in a white American culture where black voices are exiled into the peripheries of public discourse. Licorice "vigorously" attacks all competing organizations while preaching racial solidarity to boost profits for his newspaper, "which was printed by white folks and had until a year ago been full of skin-whitening and hair straightening advertisements."[17]

At its core, *Black No More* critiqued American patriotism because its colorblind rhetoric was betrayed by a coded racist vocabulary. Nowhere is this clearer than in the ostensibly competing political visions of progressive Republican Goosie and his racist Democrat challenger, Henry Givens. Paralleling Goosie's valorization of a libertarian philosophy of American nationhood "of rights of the individual and the trusts in the same paragraph" is Givens's "rugged individualism, free from the influence of sinister interests, upholding the finest ideals of honesty, independence and integrity."[18] *Black No More* showed how American patriotic arguments revolved around the universalist spectrum of American liberalism while presuming a demonized other. This is the immoral, poor, anti-American, implicitly racialized as nonwhite, who is the sacrificial lamb for which to intensify white solidarity. But *Black No More* insisted patriotism didn't need racism to realize its exclusionary potential. It could simply revise freedom to mean working under oppressive capitalism and racism as a natural right. Fisher tells white workers across the country that it was their political authority as free "citizens of the United States"[19] to prioritize their antiblack paranoia over interracial class solidarity. Likewise, a Baptist preacher equates the goal of distinctly American happiness and personal liberty, as opposed to Soviet socialism, with living under paternalistic constraints their employers impose upon them. As the preacher put its, "For what, after all is liberty except the enjoyment of life: and have they not placed within your reach those things that bring you recreation. . . . They are always thinking of you."[20]

What bothered critics of *Black No More* was that it was less a work of art, which captured something of the spirit of human complexity, and more a political treatise that didactically conveyed Schuyler's views. But this interpretation is wrong. To the contrary, *Black No More*'s use of melodrama, sensational narrative twists, and outrageous characters who were flattened of emotional depth served to hide Schuyler's own utopian hope, which he would never admit. The straw-man figure of the "true believer" Schuyler denounced in his writing could be found in the very writer of *Black No More*. He embraced interracialism and treated racial identity as a performance. *Black No More*'s opening dedication to "Caucasians in the great republic who can trace their ancestry back ten generations and confidently assert that there are no Black leaves, twigs, limbs or branches of their family trees" is retold as a fantasy through Buggerie's and Snobbcraft's failed genealogical inquiry of white people's ancestry to restrict the political rights of those who were formerly "black." Schuyler suggested that all white Americans, including "most of our social leaders," had some black ancestry and many white Americans who claimed social distinction were descendants of those who were poor and not always moral. Through this, *Black No More* mobilized a tragic narrative of US history founded on rape, enslavement, terrorism, and genocide to dethrone romantic narratives of white supremacy. As Snobbcraft says, "most of our social leaders, especially of Anglo-Saxon lineage, are descendants of colonial stock that came here in bondage. They intermixed with the blacks and the women were sexually exploited by their masters."[21] American racism creates the very conditions for its perpetuation as well as for its destruction.

At the same time, *Black No More*'s defense of racial impurity was modeled by Henry Givens's daughter, Helen. She begins the story as the racist white woman who rejects initial Disher's request for a dance. But by the conclusion, now Fisher's wife, she is relieved, rather than enraged, after discovering that her son is part black and learning of Fisher's blackness. Henry Givens's ensuing statement, "I guess we're all niggers now,"[22] expressed the American racial hybridity *Black No More* wanted readers to accept—and Schuyler realized in his own interracial marriage and family—in ways that exceeded prior black utopian calls for racial purity. Schuyler wanted Americans to know that white supremacy was nothing but a powerful fantasy, whose elimination could only be undertaken by whites. And *Black No More*'s hope was that the joy of experiencing emotional openness through interracial intimacy would replace the deadening security of racial boundaries with the vicissitudes of life.

Schuyler's utopian vision of race acknowledged the brutality of the Fordist vision of mass commodification and the automatized production process through which it was defined.[23] But *Black No More* ultimately opposed it with that of a jazz vision closer to that of the Harlem Renaissance, as an improvised performance founded on self-expression and freedom. Even if it is depicted as outside the US geographic, emotional, and cultural vocabulary, this idea is clearly captured through *Black No More*'s final image. There, we see Crookman noticing a picture in the newspaper of Fisher and his interracial son playing on a sandy beach on Cannes, France, with his wife, Helen, and her father, Henry Givens. All of them are covered in specs of sand—"quite dusty"—to blur their differences in skin-color.[24]

BLACK EMPIRE UNBOUND

Never one to pull punches, in *Black Empire* Schuyler critiques the solidification of racial identity in black, of a world where black-skin was transformed into a marker of total, authoritarian power rather than abandoned for the sake of class solidarity and reconfigured democratically. Schuyler—like many black American intellectuals at the time—was troubled by the fact that the Italian invasion of Ethiopia in 1935 was an extension of Western imperialism. But his literary response to this problem made him something of a pariah. His attempt to replace the violation of boundary crossing in *Black No More* with a critique of racial pride in *Black Empire* was seen by critics as an act of race treason. Within the rising tide of totalitarianism, there seemed to be something troubling about satirizing an anticolonial black empire that combined elements of Stalinism and Nazism. In the story, the Black Internationale, led by a charismatic yet ruthless leader, Dr. Henry Belsidus, colonizes Africa and wages a brutal war against Western Europe.

But *Black Empire* was an act not of racial loathing, but of radical critique. The novel's attack knew no bounds—black citizens as much as whites, the Euro-modern political tradition and Pan-Africanism—all while dialectically exposing the tragic dimensions of what was deemed emancipatory. *Black Empire* thus both radicalized and rendered farcical the black nationalism on display with Garvey in the 1920s that Schuyler consistently rejected. And it undermined white supremacist narratives of black political passivity. *Black Empire* gave reality to the utopian potential of black power by representing black people as agents in their destiny and racial identity as a source of resistance. But it simultaneously raised an alarm about its costs through a counterintuitive argument. Insofar as elites became repressive dictators and race became the justification for unspeakable violence,[25] the black utopian imagination would be susceptible to inegalitarian American cultural thinking.[26]

Black Empire implicated as exclusionary a prominent strain of American realism—from James Madison, Alexander Hamilton,

Martin Delany, and Malcolm X. This tradition argued that ends-based thinking devoid of any moral considerations was serviceable in a real world saturated by historically conditioned inequality. But for Schuyler, this had the effect of authorizing a self-referential power that knew no checks and bounds. Belsidus's justification of global black empire as something that couldn't be judged by moral standards but only by political effectiveness expressed *Black Empire*'s concern that political "reality" (i.e., necessary, natural common sense) was an open term subject to monopolization by arbitrary power. As Belsidus says, "I have dedicated my life, Slater, to destroying white supremacy. . . . I plan to do this by every means within my power. . . . Indeed . . . there can be no talk of right or wrong. Right is success. Wrong is failure."[27] In *Black Empire*'s narrative, the intertwined paternalism and ethnocentric myopia that had plagued Enlightenment universalism morphs into a version of black power. It demands certainty, not ambivalence; closure, not openness; consolidation, not dissolution. This makes stillborn the possibility of popular rule. Belsidus says, "We will recondition the Negro masses in accordance with the most approved behavioristic methods,"[28] and wonders, "what are a few paltry lives compared to the goal we seek? . . . Haven't they murdered millions of black people?"[29] Belsidus disregards the intrinsic worth of all human beings in favor of a brutal instrumental logic turned genocidal in his defense of murder for the sake of a larger good. He exemplified *Black Empire*'s claim that arbitrary power evacuated commitments central to utopian freedom: that of justice, where all are treated fairly and with dignity, and the rule of law, which protects dissent and minority rights.

Although Belsidus was no political liberal, he expressed *Black Empire*'s penetrating critique of the way American liberalism stifled black freedom dreams within the United States and, consequently, promoted black nationalist ideology. As he put it, "We must disobey all laws that hinder our plan, for all laws here are laws of the white men, designed to keep us in subjugation and perpetuate his rule."[30] Belsidus claims what Garvey insisted and Du Bois began to believe in the 1930s: liberalism defends individualism but doesn't address structural oppression; liberalism champions the rule of law, but its pretense to universalism never grants the oppressed the authority to achieve its benefits. Belsidus's belief in realistic self-preservation—his view that the South only understands "force," and that war is necessary for peace[31]—implicates in domination modern political thought's emphasis upon the importance of security, the inescapability of competition, and rational self-interest.[32] To be sure, early in his life Schuyler was an avowed militarist who spent six years in the army before becoming jaded by its racism. But *Black Empire* was an antiwar text, which connected the endgame of factional competition not to the preservation of liberty, but to total war. Belsidus's argument that "The South and those who rule it understand only one thing: force" leads to the conclusion that "we shall repay violence with violence, burning with burning, death by death."[33] This is expressed through Belsidus's success at inflaming racial tensions between Jews, Catholics, and Protestants to distract them from the Internationale's politics. The Internationale's enactment of black power perfects not democracy, but the instruments of mass destruction and extermination—everything from plague carrying rats to corrosive acid, from the extermination of millions of whites in Africa to the construction of a so-called death ray.

Relatedly, *Black Empire* rejected a narrow view of freedom based on capitalism and scientific advancement, which combined the talented elite black citizens with the scientific rationality of "intellectuals, scientists, engineers," and "money, instruments, new weapons of science"[34] at the expense of the black majority. Although Schuyler himself often embraced Eurocentric narratives about the primacy of Western civilization, *Black Empire* denounced progressive narratives of liberal development, which saw people of color as insufficiently ready for freedom by suggesting that it simply re-created the racism from which black people wished to escape—"Africa is still far behind," Belsidus says at one point.[35] But at the same time, *Black Empire* was suspicious of Afrocentric civilizational uplift narratives. Rev. Binks's the Church of Love is founded by the Internationale as an alternative spiritual philosophy to white Christianity, but is betrayed by the sole objective of preserving the Internationale's colonial mission. Binks says,

> You will realize that black people can only become great, black people can only become prosperous, black people can only become powerful by loving one another. It must be a wholehearted, unashamed, literal love which black people have from henceforth for one another. Loving each other, my people, we must therefore help each other. We must not quarrel or contend with each other.[36]

Binks's attempt to join black exceptionalism to black self-love and his valorization of black community illustrates the way love's radical challenge to self-interest would be sacrificed when linked to the narrow goal of prosperity, how its defense of dignity could become subsumed under the task of national greatness, its idealism distorted by its realism, its expansive possibilities effaced by its immersion in politics.

Love became dangerous in yet another way in *Black Empire*. Not simply by justifying the Internationale's internal policing of dissent of what it presumes are counterrevolutionaries, but becoming the basis for eugenics. Slater and Givens are horrified when they are shown the medical facilities in the new black empire, which are meant to perfect the black race. They are told not only that disabled people are a drain upon society, but that ending their suffering is "quite sensible and altogether humane."[37] In this way, Schuyler denounced utopian social perfection. In his view, eliminating imperfection to achieve human advancement concealed power inequities that determined who counted as worthwhile. The novel revealed how one of liberalism's founding wishes to minimize suffering led to maximal violence. Utilitarian considerations about the greatest happiness for the most people give little room for treating individuals as ends. Natural rights or morality are no longer the standard by which action is judged as humane. Humaneness became measured by the standard of reasonableness and normalcy, which is determined by dominant groups.

Social perfection in utopian thought had always conjured the question of gender. Though few would describe Schuyler as a committed feminist, *Black Empire* dramatized gender equality and described it as threatened by the political theory upon which black power rested. Slater's desire to possess Givens—who is a pilot and intellectual leader of the Internationale—is *Black Empire*'s warning that masculine desire could be an extension of, and easily intersect with, the instrumental attitude behind revolutionary political projects. Slater says, "Men and women are on a plane of equality. Social and economic difference between the sexes have become a thing of the past. . . . Life has been made too complex, and man was intended to live a life of simplicity. . . . Because of her probable desire not to settle down into wifely domesticity, I was held off."[38] Slater's frustration at repressing feelings of natural sexual difference and yearning for a nostalgic age of male domination insulates him from feminist critique.

Likewise, Belsidus's redescription of womanhood as irrational, far too practical, and lacking ingenuity eliminates a powerful source of immanent social critique. The realization of political equality never addresses the toxicity of unbridled male desire. Belsidus's objection to marriage on the basis that women, like "spiders," are naturally possessive and exploiting of their male partners in ways that erode male individuality and "are incurably sentimental, essentially petty and lacking in true idealism"[39] reveales how diminished masculine self-worth would find a home in an authoritarian movement that promises future male power. Black utopia couldn't escape the way misogynistic myths of sentimental womanhood justified woman's subordination. The ingredients necessary to keep the spirit of utopian liberation alive would be expunged by the practical demands of maintaining and consolidating political power.

Black Empire's concluding lesson was much like *Black No More*'s: that the utopia of racial purity not only perpetuated the repression it sought to escape, but repressed its fear of vulnerability, of living in the messiness that characterized democratic life and its failure to extend radical social critique to emancipatory rule. This point was made clear in the novel's concluding account of a thwarted lynching, which paralleled *Black No More*'s. Givens and Slater make an emergency landing in a small village in the jungle of Northern Sierra Leone, only to be approached by black cannibals who intend to eat them alive. If the lynching of Snobbcraft and Buggerie was Schuyler's representation of the way skin color doesn't protect one from the underlying violence, instrumentalism, and acquisitive individualism upon which white supremacy rests, then Slater's words, "What irony, what bitter irony that we, who had risked so much for the liberation of black people, should come to our death at the hands of black people!,"[40] convey the consequence of antidemocratic black power that didn't examine its commitment to scientific rationality, its vision of civilizational progress, its belief in thinking where the ends justifies the means, and gender inequality.

SATIRE, REVERENCE, AND REACTION

Schuyler's nonconformist spirit made him do everything in his power to desanctify utopia. Utopia conjures images of reverent idealism, intellectual consistency, and moral certitude. Satire, in contrast, embodies a spirit of irreverent playfulness, where truths are constantly being exposed for what they conceal. Schuyler devoted his writings in the 1930s to stressing this split. But perhaps his antiutopian criticism also led him astray politically in ways that he couldn't have possibly imagined. He transformed from a committed egalitarian to a ruthless conservative, from someone who cared deeply about expanding freedom for the many to someone who made company with racists, reactionaries, and militarists. Indeed, Schuyler's ideological transformation may have emerged from his lifelong iconoclasm. Nothing was more unfashionable than simultaneously decrying black nationalist race pride, white racial liberalism, and black progressivism in the 1920s. And nothing was more controversial than assuming the mantle of black conservatism in the 1960s when the vision of black equality Schuyler defended throughout his life was being realized through the civil rights movement. Strikingly, a central influence of the movement was none other than Schuyler's one-time friend, A. Philip Randolph, who once hired him for his magazine, *Messenger*.

Whatever explained Schuyler's politics, his literary antiutopianism was centered on a radical critique of American cultural mythologies many conservatives and liberals alike couldn't accept. The charge of anti-Americanism Schuyler would level against hippies, feminists, socialists, communists, and black power in the 1960s could have easily been directed toward his work in the 1930s. Reading his work, one gets the sense that little is valuable in a utopia that can't imagine a future of economic equality, gender liberation, popular democracy, nonviolence, and peace. In the 1930s, this never came about in America. In fact, it was being visibly expunged in Stalinist Russia and Nazi Germany. But the intensity of Schuyler's satires betrayed his lifelong nonchalance and realism. It revealed instead someone who wanted citizens to appreciate how utopia could be distorted and how it might be reclaimed.

5

RICHARD WRIGHT'S *BLACK POWER* AND ANTICOLONIAL ANTIUTOPIANISM

The first best-selling black American writer, Richard Wright (1908–60), left his exiled life in Paris to visit the British Gold Coast colony in 1953, which would ultimately become the independent African nation of Ghana under the leadership of Kwame Nkrumah and his Convention People's Party. He did this to understand the nature of its anticolonial independence movement. Wright was not alone in his interest. During the 1950s and 1960s, Ghana seemed like a utopian space for many black American expat intellectuals. Du Bois, Julian Mayfield, St. Claire Drake, and Maya Angelou lived there at some point and used it as a foundation for developing a transnational notion of antiracist citizenship beyond the US-centered civil rights movement.[1] But what Wright found and later chronicled in his travelogue in the Gold Coast, *Black Power: A Record of Reactions in a Land of Pathos* (1954) was something different, which both troubled and reframed his understanding of global black life. Wright wrote, "I wanted the opportunity to try to weigh a movement like this. . . . It was the first time in my life that I'd come in contact with a mass movement conducted by Negro leadership."[2] Always an intellectual rebel, Wright was uninterested in superimposing American ideas onto the African continent like Delany or treating it as a geographic fix for black

FIGURE 5.1 Richard Wright. Library of Congress, Prints and Photographs Division, Carl Van Vechten Collection, LC-USZ62–42502.

American exploitation like Garvey. Wright came to Africa not to validate US democracy, but to deconstruct it by considering what futuristic lessons the African liberation struggle might have for American political thinking. And yet, what began as a journey toward greater intellectual clarification soon became for Wright a chronicle of confusion. His disbelief at what he saw as the dystopian level of poverty and suffering was only matched by his surprise at what he saw as the troubling infusion of traditional African folk culture into the sphere of political rule and social life, undermining future Ghanaian citizens' capacity for self-determination.[3]

For these reasons, *Black Power* has been read as a marginal work in Wright's opus or as an embarrassment to his legacy. For some, it was a free-flowing, stream-of-consciousness record of Wright's naïve anthropological musings, juxtaposed against his emotional navel-gazing. From this view, *Black Power* gained in self-disclosure what it lacked in theoretical rigor and sophistication. For others, it was a vociferous—at times, almost unnecessarily so—denigration of African people and customs. Many insisted that what the text lacked in analysis it gained in rhetorical malice.[4]

But *Black Power* was much more than critics appreciated and what Wright himself declared. It was a key part of the black utopian tradition. After all, Wright's very disappointment with the Gold Coast contained a meditation on the unraveling of his utopian hope of Africa becoming the last beacon for dismantling white supremacist thought. Paradoxically, by trying to outline the practical ways in which the Gold Coast could become a republic capable of competing on the global stage, Wright lost sight of the way *Black Power* was itself an unconscious catalogue. It was something of a waking daydream, of how to accomplish this differently in a way that created a postcolonial society unmoored from the political theory of Western colonialism.

DEMOCRATIC AMBIVALENCE AND RADICAL SELF-CRITICISM

Wright's antiutopianism in his naturalist fiction and Marxist politics stemmed from his lifelong commitment to realism. This was informed by his early life of poverty in Mississippi and his later intellectual immersion in and friendship with the "Chicago School" sociologists Horace Clayton and Louis Wirth, whose research privileged data-driven socioeconomic explanations over normative judgments.[5] Wright's intellectual orientation was expressed in *Black Power*'s delineation of a strict opposition between dreams and reality. Dreams, for him, were the apolitical realm of fantasy, immaturity, and unconscious desire. Reality, in contrast, was that of strategy, rule, and government.

But this very opposition was betrayed by Wright's unconscious investment in psychoanalysis. He invoked traditional categories associated with the preeminent figure in the field, Sigmund Freud, such as the "return of the repressed," projection, introjection, phobia, and taboo.[6] Moreover, *Black Power*'s introductory internal monologue detailed a political version of Freud's utopian vision of self-knowledge. Wright's free-associative process shattered the myth of sovereign arbitrary power and dichotomizing reasoning upon which colonialism subsisted.[7] Reflecting on his own uncertainty about his connection to Africa, Wright found nothing satisfying in the allure of absolute truth or binaries. This is because they limited the sense of political possibility that an orientation based on ambiguity provided. Wright wrote, "I refuse to make a religion out of that which I do not know. I too can feel the limit of my reactions, can feel where my puny self ends, can savor the terror of it. . . . I don't know. *Must* I know that?"[8] This was Wright's overarching mantra in *Black Power* for capturing the theoretical power of ambivalence—of confusion, fallibility, contingency. Such an orientation unleashed deeper questions about the self. It had the potential for revising what one believed and how one acted. This was not simply Wright's aesthetic act of self-reinvention or stoic nonchalance, but an embodiment of anticolonial political theorizing.[9]

Experience, which was itself a site of contestation and involved competing perceptions, or what Nietzsche called "perspectivalism," was for Wright a necessary condition for political thinking. His questions—Was he African or not? How could he know a country he had never set foot on? What was the link between his black identity and that of Africans?—replaced the Euro-modern utopian trope of the "noble savage" with a rigorous deconstruction of one's identity. And it made radical skepticism into an ethical mantra. As Wright put it, "I'm African! I'm of African descent. . . . Yet I'd never seen Africa; I'd never really known any Africans; I'd hardly ever thought of Africa. . . . Africa was a vast continent full of 'my people.' . . . Or had three hundred years imposed a psychological distance between me and the 'racial stock' from which I had sprung? . . . But my emotions seemed to be touching a dark and dank wall. . . . *But, am I African?*"[10] Such dizzying self-examination and endless questioning were an honest account of his transition from his unreconstructed understanding of "black identity," as it dramatized his view that critique exploded the ideological ground upon which one stood.

Throughout the text, Wright's conviction in a shared, universal black experience was replaced with a sense of cultural, geographical, and historical difference. Displayed here was a political version of the existentialism that Wright both learned from and taught through his fiction to the likes of Jean-Paul Sartre, Simon de Beauvoir, and Albert Camus in France in the 1950s, where he lived in exile from the United States. For Wright, political clarity emerged from being exposed to different perspectives of strangers one hadn't encountered.[11] Wright shifted his gaze from the position of sovereign critic to receptive observer. The "Africans" that were fictionalized in the colonial imagination were given texture. Their complex humanity was laid bare in ways that many twentieth-century Africana philosophers—Leopold

Senghor, Aimé Césaire, and Alioune Diop—believed gave proof to a unique cultural specificity and intellectual orientation. This idea, of "negritude," asserted that Africana thought was defined by the values of communalism, humanism, social pluralism.[12] Given Wright's obvious awareness of cultural pluralism, it was ironic that he was such a vociferous critic of negritude. He opposed it for the same reason he opposed the philosophy of Alain Locke and the literature of the Harlem Renaissance generally. He believed it applied a singular spiritual quality to a heterogeneous black diaspora and replaced rational class analysis with racial essentialism.[13]

Nonetheless, Wright's perspectivalism opened a competing line of vision from Senghor. What he saw in the Gold Coast was not black cultural resilience, but instead what his friend the Martiniquan psychiatrist Frantz Fanon believed was the European colonial domination that distorted black identity. As Wright put it, "the Western assumption of the inferiority of the African compels the Westerner to constrict the African's environment, so, in time, . . . what was, in the beginning, merely a false assumption, become a reality."[14] For Wright, colonialism created the civic education that destroyed the youthful innocence of the love, joy, excitement, risk, and experimentation necessary for utopian dreams. "Maybe," he wondered, "that was why one seldom encountered what might be called 'idealism' in Africa?"[15]

But *Black Power* paralleled the negritude movement's questioning of the normative assumptions about what counted as morally valuable and politically necessary. Wright wondered, "Was Africa 'primitive'? But what did being 'primitive' mean? . . . I was dismayed to discover that I didn't know how to react to it."[16] His ambivalence toward the definition of "primitive" expressed his rejection of singular notions of political time—Who gets to decide when something is right or ready? In this way, Wright placed power in the uncomfortable position to account for its validity. Authority over political claim-making became an open question. This allowed him to turn narratives of civilization on their head. The goal of "civilization" was exposed in Wright's skilled hands as inhumane and violent. Wright announced in theory what *Black Empire* only speculated about in fiction. If colonial rulers exemplified the apogee of civilization, then emulating them would promote terror, rather than liberation. He asked, "What do you call ready? Are people civilized and ready to govern themselves when they become so desperate that they put a knife at the throat of their rulers?"[17]

This recognition prompted Wright to seriously question his own standpoint. He modeled an exemplary kind of critical awareness of his Eurocentric political reasoning, exploding its universalism. He lay bare how his judgments about development were determined by a Marxist worldview that he had inherited from his early romance with the US Communist Party. As much as anything else, *Black Power* chronicled the way Wright's own position as interpreter was chastened, his conviction about value revised. As he wondered, "I began to question, *my* assumptions. I was assuming that these people had to be pulled out of this life, out of these conditions of poverty, had to become literate and eventually industrialized. But why? Was not the desire for that mostly on my part rather than theirs?"[18]

Still, Wright never went far enough. His laudatory acknowledgment of his intellectual limitations didn't involve a complete reconsideration of them.[19] He fell prey to his own unexamined homophobia and faith in hierarchical masculinity, which were betrayed by his support of queer writers like James Baldwin and black women writers like Margaret Walker. He expressed "uneasiness" of "emotion deeper" than he "could control" at boys holding hands in the streets and justified the patriarchal family and tribal structure of African life.[20] Though Wright's association with de Beauvoir immersed him in a world of second-wave philosophic feminism, in which womanhood was dialectically defined and made subservient through its antithesis to manhood, his offhand assessment of sex workers as the "only real democrats within reach" sounded off-key—less like a 1960s sex-positive endorsement of black women's agency as workers autonomously controlling their labor and more like an oversight of the unequal status of women's commodification under patriarchy.[21]

CONTRADICTIONS OF FREEDOM

Wright's self-analysis expressed his preoccupation with freedom, which was at the center of his concerns and that of the African liberation struggle. This was precisely the underlying question of *Black Power*: What does it mean to be free? And after witnessing a rally in which Nkrumah was cheered by his supporters with chants of "free—doom" over and over again, Wright began to develop an answer:

> But here in Africa "freedom" was more than a word; an African had no doubts about the meaning of the word "freedom." It meant the right to public assembly, the right to physical movement, the right to make known his views, the right to elect men of his choice to public office, and the right to recall them if they failed in their promises. At a time when the Western world grew embarrassed at the sound of the word "freedom," these people knew that it meant the right to shape their own destiny as they wished. Of

> that they had no doubt, and no threats could intimidate them about it; they might be cowed by guns and planes, but they'd not change their minds about the concrete nature of the freedom that they wanted and were willing to die for.[22]

Without question, *Black Power*'s rhetorical structure as a blend of memoir, political critique, and travelogue obscured Wright's view of freedom. But this careful meditation on what freedom meant to Africans suggested that, for him, it was something more expressive and expansive than was developed by the NAACP political strategy of litigation for political enfranchisement. Wright saw freedom as a lived experience dependent upon but irreducible to certain political rights. It was about shaping one's destiny without another's say, a new beginning in which one would identify what counted as meaningful.

Wright only glimpsed what Malcolm X fully articulated in the year before his death after visiting Ghana in 1964: the African concept of freedom gave the African the ability to develop their personality beyond white European constraints. As Malcolm put, "his concept of freedom is a situation or a condition in which he, as an African, feels completely free to give vent to his own likes and dislikes and thereby develop his own African personality."[23] Malcolm saw in Africa what Wright didn't. After he arrived back to the United States, Malcolm was transformed from a spokesperson for Elijah Muhammad and the Nation of Islam into a defender of democratic struggles and human rights. For him, narrow national solutions to racism were ultimately flawed in their myopic particularism. For these reasons, Malcolm urged citizens to see the global dimensions of racism, where problems treated as particular to a national culture needed to be seen as linked to broader liberation struggles. Transforming the focus from black civil rights to human rights reframed white supremacy as a deprivation of basic humanity and globalized black American political problems.

Though Wright did not leave the Gold Coast with the same theoretical transformation, he nonetheless anticipated Malcolm's view that the meaning of freedom for racially oppressed citizens came from what they were deprived of. The dialectic between the "doom" one experienced under colonialism and the utopia of being "free" in the recurrent chants was reconfigured. For Wright, domination gave rise to the knowledge that freedom was precarious and needed vigilance. He found a political theory embedded within the chanting and dancing of Nkrumah's supporters about reaching the Promised Land. Static images of community based on blood were temporally suspended and replaced with improvisation through the rhythmic dancing of Nkrumah's women supporters. They were "doing a sort of weaving, circular motion[,] their bodies . . . in a quiet, physical manner, . . . as if only the total movement of their entire bodies could indicate in some measure their acquiescence, their surrender, their approval."[24] In this sense, Wright saw how a community came from a kind of immanent presence, founded upon certain, evolving commitments.

Strikingly, however, Wright couldn't appreciate what he described so vividly as a systematic anticolonial Africana philosophy. This philosophy combined elements of Nkrumah's "African socialism," which sought to reconcile Marxist economic equality with the lived communal traditions of African peoples, or Senghor's, which said, "power—is founded on spiritual and democratic laws. . . . Decisions of all kinds are deliberated in a *palaver*. . . . Work is shared out among the sexes. . . . This is a community based society."[25] Wright's unwillingness to appreciate this counterhegemonic mode of thought was striking precisely because Senghor saw Wright's work, especially his autobiography, *Black Boy* (1945), as a formative influence in his political thought.[26] Indeed, even when Wright praised Senghor's interpretation of African poetry at the First Conference for Negro Artists and Writers in Paris (1956), in which they both spoke, he implicated black religion—and by extension "negritude"—as complicit for colonial rule.[27]

All this explained why Wright felt an overwhelming sense of dread and anxiety in his reluctance to partake in the traditional dance and song between Nkrumah and his supporters. He asked: "How much am I a part of this? How much was I part of it when I saw it in America? Why could I not feel this? Why that peculiar, awkward restraint when I tried to dance or sing?"[28] Rather than ask what this experience could teach him, it opened up for him an exploration about the contradictions of postcolonial rule. For Wright, the vibrant energy that made freedom so meaningful, dynamic, and worth fighting for was what escaped institutionalization. But recognizing freedom in the political world required certain boundaries between rulers and ruled, which could be problematically collapsed in the course of its pursuit. As Wright explained, "At times the dialogue between the speaker and the audience is so intimate, so prolonged, so dramatic that all sense of distance between leaders and followers ceased to exist, and a spirit of fellowship, of common identity prevailed among faces young and old, smooth and bearded, wise and simple. . . . The speaker lifted his voice in song and the mass joined in, and the collective sound seemed to rise as high as the skies."[29] This was one of Wright's central antiutopian critiques. There was a tension between the fact that popular voice needed to find a home in leaders for building a new polity and the fact that leaders needed to recognize that their authority was always fractured and compromised. He described the relationship between

Nkrumah and his supporters as "politics plus . . . involve[ing] a total and basic response to reality; it smacked of the dreamlike, of the stuff of which art and myths were made."[30] And by doing so, he uprooted politics from the rationality it professed and highlighted what it obscured. This was the dialectic of democratic engagement driven toward emancipation—of speaking and listening, expressing desire and interest, the call and response—which became an art, couched in myth and symbol.

Wright remained convinced that this dynamic could not address the problem of pluralism: "What would happen to a romantic rebel in an African tribe," he wondered, when "all other dreams are bared, are taboo?"[31] But in mistakenly denigrating the nonrational elements of traditional culture Wright couldn't appreciate the way its symbolism contained a philosophy that challenged the orthodoxy of Western systems that promoted inequality. Here is how Wright interpreted the story of a religious man speaking of his desire for a ritualistic burial, which included his friends watching black ants (called "God's slaves") go over his coffin and taking one of these ants, which symbolized the soul of the dead man, to be buried next to his ancestors:

> These, of course, are but dreams, daylight dreams, dreams dreamed with the eyes wide open! Was it that the jungle, so rich, so fertile, was it that life, so warm, so filled with ready food, so effortless, prompted men to dream dreams likes this? Or was it the opposite? These dreams belong to the African; they existed before the coming of the white man. . . . It may be, of course, that dreams are the staunchest kind of reality. . . . It may be that such beliefs fit the soul of man better than railroads, mass productions, wars. . . . All men, in some form or other, love these dreams. Maybe men are happier when they are wrapped in warm dreams of being with their fathers when they die?[32]

Had Wright taken seriously the diverse epistemic claims of African philosophy, which challenged the Cartesian dualism between mind and body, and privileged communalism over individualism, he might have had a different interpretation of the dream. He might have seen, for instance, that the American rugged individualism that Wright himself lamented was replaced here with a sense of community, that friendship replaced the competition and war Wright abhorred, that dignity replaced the idea of monolithic capitalist development. Wright's denunciation of the African "tribal mind" as "sensuous; loving images, not concepts; personalities, not abstractions; movement, not form; dreams, not reality"[33] missed not only the way that these binaries were false in both Afro and Euro philosophy, but also that this very reasoning wouldn't as readily support the thoughtlessness and economic exploitation of colonialism.[34] In *Black Power*, Wright thus committed the same mistake he did in his long-form essay, *12 Million Black Voices* (1941), which served as an accompaniment to Edwin Rosskam's photos of everyday black people—sharecroppers, churchgoers, city inhabitants—struggling to survive.[35] In both texts, he exclusively focused his eye on the structural conditions that explained the injustice he experienced without giving full texture to the philosophy being generated through resistance to it.

ABANDONING CRITIQUE, DISAVOWING UTOPIA

Ultimately, Wright's investment in conceptualizing black liberation through a Western European model haunted the final section of *Black Power*. Wright's concluding prescription to Nkrumah to be "hard"[36] and to "militarize" "the social lives of the people, . . . [to] unite the nation, sweep out the tribal cobwebs, and place the feet of the masses upon a basis of reality,"[37] stemmed from his view that Ghanaian national identity was undeveloped. His anxiety about the return of global imperialism led him to embrace an antidemocratic ethos that was arguably as dystopian as the Gold Coast society created by it. As he wondered, "But suppose I didn't?," Wright reflected, speaking of his desire for bringing Gold Coast citizens into the fold of Western industrialization, "What would happen then? They would remain in these slavelike conditions forever. . . . The British would continue to suck their blood."[38] Clearly, his concern that black liberation would fail without proper Western measures was occasioned by a sense not of superiority but of practicality, not by the wish for exploitation but as an act of solidarity. Still, Wright's utopian hope of an equal and free black diaspora was replaced with the recognition that Euro-modern political thought would have to be prioritized above all else. As he wrote, in words that made him sound more utopian than the realist he imagined himself to be, "the Western world has one last opportunity in Africa to determine if its ideals can be generously shared, if it dares to act upon its deepest convictions. . . . Now has come Africa's turn to test the ideals that the West has preached but failed to practice."[39] Strength and certainty became Wright's antidote to the ambivalence and vulnerability embodied in his own free-associative process and the lived experience of Ghanaian culture. Consequently, when Wright urged Nkrumah to "feel free to improvise," it was in the service of freeing Ghanaians of "mumbo-jumbo," rather than recognizing the spirit of improvisation already evident in their lives.[40]

Two years later, *Black Power*'s concluding thoughts were given a testing ground in Wright's *The Color Curtain* (1956). This later text chronicled his attendance at the Bandung Conference in

Indonesia in 1955 that saw the leadership of twenty-nine African and Asian nations gathering to discuss possibilities for antiracist solidarity. *The Color Curtain* vividly revealed Wright's own utopianism of global socialism, rationalism, modernization, and elite vanguard political rule, while lamenting the very thing he diagnosed in *Black Power*—the mysticism, lack of focus, and concerted strategy in Ghana were on display in Bandung.[41]

Black Power was forgotten, if not deliberately ignored, when Wright died suddenly in 1960. Ironically, the year of his death was the same year in which there was a wave of independence throughout the African continent in countries like Congo, Cameroon, Senegal, and Nigeria. In retrospect, Wright would be remembered for his groundbreaking depiction of the tragedy of urban black life, for his political involvements—from communism to Marxism and radical liberalism—and for paving the way for a generation of postwar black writers, of which Ralph Ellison, Margaret Walker, and James Baldwin were the best known. For many observers, his novel *Native Son* (1940) was Wright's clearest statement of his political philosophy, which fictionalized the way racist socioeconomic exploitation fused with an unjust criminal justice system deprived black citizens—as expressed through *Native Son*'s protagonist, Bigger Thomas—of the possibility of dreaming for a world that was not defined by racial domination.[42] But it was perhaps *Black Power* that saw Wright—however ambivalently and strenuously—struggling to articulate something of his own utopian hope, his aspiration for the possibility of global black liberation.

6

SUN RA AND COSMIC BLACKNESS

Herman Blount, who would more famously be known as Le Sony'r Ra, or "Sun Ra" (1914–93), was a twentieth-century pioneer in avant-garde jazz composition and performance. He saw his inheritance in the long tradition of black musicians like Bessie Smith, Ida Cox, Ethel Waters, Duke Ellington, and Charlie Parker. But his otherworldly philosophical musings suffused with a metaphysical exploration of human existence linked him to the black utopian tradition.[1] No figure before Ra had so thoroughly sanctified the concept of utopia and imagined it in a way that was virtually unrecognizable and unrealizable. And no one had defined it with such moral seriousness in ways that were so obscure and contradictory.

Ra's provocative suggestion was not that black people needed to immigrate or assimilate, but that they needed to undertake space travel in search of new planets. Within the context of the black utopian tradition, his view was much like the music produced by his band, the Arkestra. It was by turns striking, unsettling, and thought-provoking—collapsing distinctions between fact and fiction, belief and imagination. But what Ra thought was a matter of absolute consistency, critics treated as a blatant contradiction. Many celebrated Ra's noncommercial, underground Afro-modern music for its blend of Afro-beat, gospel,

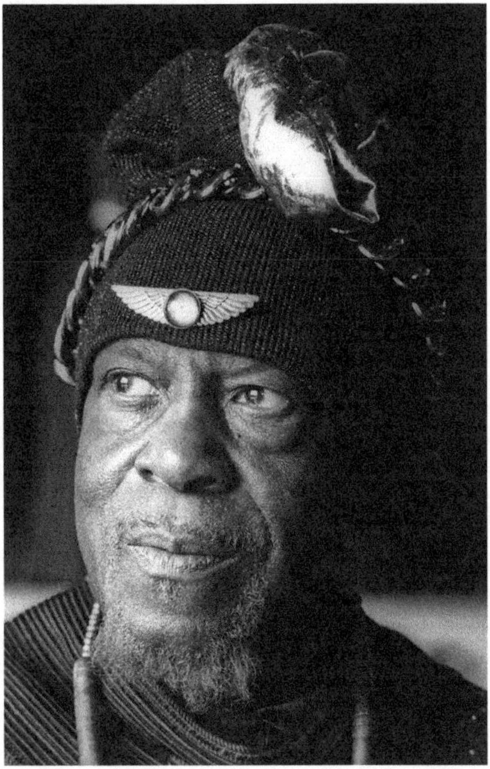

FIGURE 6.1 Sun Ra. marc marnie/Alamy Stock Photo.

blues, funk, and jazz. No doubt, there was something revolutionary in his attempt to fuse the stylized cool of a Miles Davis with Wagnerian epic, to mix the atonalism of an Arnold Schoenberg with the experimental repetitions and silences of a John Cage and Philip Glass. To move from past to present, across cultures and between sounds that were, by turns, euphoric and nightmarish, transcendent and haunting. But many critics derided what they perceived as Ra's embarrassing personal eccentricities. For them, his combination of mysticism, poetic reasoning, and aphoristic quotations—as well as highly stylized public persona as someone who was *from* but not *of* this world—merely diminished his art. This made him less the artistic genius he was and more of a charlatan, if not trickster. Many were entertained by his presence. Some were transformed by his sounds. But very few wanted to listen to what Ra had to say.

This reputation was further entrenched when Ra refused to sanctify Martin Luther King after his death, and went so far as to say that the civil rights movement was a lost cause because it didn't achieve its promise of social transformation, despite a decade-long struggle. During the years of Republican Ronald Reagan's presidency in the 1980s, Ra expressed unrelenting pessimism about what he was earlier intrigued by in the 1960s. This was his faith in the political potential of black art in forging a new consciousness, which he learned through his involvement in black intellectual and artistic circles in New York and Chicago. As he put it an interview in 1983, "What [civil rights leaders] were talking about may have been correct, but the advances—the so-called advances that darker people have made in America, that was cut off by Reagan. So, really, what good was [King's] death?"[2]

On the surface, Ra's act of self-making, relaying his story of being abducted and taken on a spaceship to another planet, seemed to give evidence of his conviction in political withdrawal. As if his only concern was to embrace art for art's sake. This was the idea popularized by the black novelist Ralph Ellison in the 1950s and rejected by black radicals associated with the Black Arts Movement like the poet Amiri Baraka in the 1960s. In a certain sense, Ra's metaphysical speculations about the unknown reaches of the cosmos had the hallmarks of the kind of religious asceticism that Nietzsche once denounced as part of the "slave morality," which expressed resignation to power, rather than seizing it as a terrain to be confronted.[3] From this interpretation, it would seem Ra depoliticized the pessimism that energized earlier utopians' call for broadening black politics beyond the US nation-state—whether through emigration or political solidarity with the Global South.

But this assessment is not entirely accurate because, as with utopian thought generally, Ra's art exceeded his own political commitments. Though they have largely been ignored as sources of political critique, his narratives of escape and transcendence, coupled with his eclectic philosophical orientation of Afro-mythology and cosmic worldview, paved a futuristic orientation at odds with structures of thought that sustained US racial domination.[4]

REMIXING AMERICA, REIMAGINING BLACKNESS

Ra's aesthetic was political. His wardrobe blended a spacesuit with the royal garb of the pharaoh and he renamed himself. Both decisions played on and embodied an ancient, romanticized Egyptian mythologized black past, which he learned about through reading George James's *Stolen Legacy* (1954). Ra acknowledged this activity as a self-conscious form of "myth-making," which gave normative value to denigrated blackness. For this reason, when Ra privileged what he called "mythocracy" above "democracy," it was not to denigrate popular rule, but it was to argue for blending Nietzsche's notion of the "will to power" with poststructural arguments that truth was a narrative. He insisted, "Reality equals death, because everything which is real has a beginning and an end. Myth speaks of the impossible, of immortality. And since everything that's possible has been tried, we need to try to the impossible."[5] At stake for Ra was not reclaiming antidemocratic conservative hierarchy. But it was exposing the way democratic values like freedom and justice were co-opted by power historically. Turning to myth provided Ra a frame from which to contest hegemonic ideas.

To this end, few things preoccupied Ra more than cultivating a futuristic language unconstrained by prior expectations. His aim was to deconstruct binaries of racial meaning, moral virtue, and abjection. Although Ra never had academic training in the poststructural tradition, he clearly understood the power of semiotics. This was expressed through the syllabus of the course he taught as an adjunct at University of California, Berkeley, in 1971, called "The Black Man in the Cosmos." The elasticity of language meant it could be remade. In his course, Ra had students engage questions of class, negritude, and technology in music. They had to think culture not through Eurocentric sources, but through a mix of folklore, ancient Egyptian hieroglyphics, and ex-slaves' writing. Ra put biblical equations on the board and rewrote them into new meanings, as new chains of signifiers.[6]

His aim to resignify meaning explained why Ra consistently called enslaved people in the United States "angels" for brutally laboring in the fields. This was not to romanticize or sanctify their suffering, but to reclaim the existence of black dignity beyond the experience of commodification under racial capitalism.[7] Ra's insistence upon using jarring descriptions—for him, black people were "aliens," and nonblack Americans were "niggers"—was not driven by perpetuating sensationalized narratives of absolute otherness within an established community or to mobilize racism against itself. But instead, it was about defamiliarizing established meanings of American nationalism.[8] For instance, by insisting in a 1988 concert that "nigger" was etymologically derived from the Hebrew word *ger*, which meant "stranger," Ra sought to universalize the history of immigration and alienation common to the American experience. His goal was less about creating moral equivalence between the injustices experienced by white ethnics and black slaves. To the contrary, it was about transforming American nationhood from an organic entity into a constellation of forces defined by vulnerability, difference, and dissonance.[9]

Ra's claim that he knew more about the segregated experience of black lives in the United States than white people was laudable but not quite accurate. He was keenly aware of the ironies of American liberalism. The poetic speaker in Ra's poem "The Delusion Freedom" questioned the value of liberty amid famine, calling into question its transcendent universal promise, founded in God's vision of human equality, within the backdrop of war. As he put it, "What good is freedom's liberty / If sword and famine and pestilence / Is its creed. . . . It is according to / That which is written / As proclaimed word of God / To those to whom it was given: / An unfailingly promised heritage."[10] Ra rejected epistemological frameworks that professed universality and championed human dignity—whether Christianity, liberalism, or realism—but were linked to global capitalism, the plundering of the Earth and the rationalization of exploitation.[11] In 1942, he was jailed for refusing to report to mandatory community service after his pacifism led him to become a conscientious objector to World War II. This experience must have informed his view that the distinction between justice and injustice, right and wrong, was collapsed by power. For this reason, Ra continued black utopianism's critique of the rule of law as formalizing, rather than challenging, inequality. His poem "Calling Planet Earth" declared, "You can go to jail for doing / wrong. / You can go to jail for doing right. / You can go to jail for doing nothing."[12] Ra's critique of American culture was more political than existential. This is why—although he visited and debated with them in Chicago, where their main offices were located just blocks from his recording studio—Ra disagreed with Elijah Muhammad and the Nation of Islam's wholesale rebuke of white people as devils.

For Ra, the lack of social consciousness that American thought had long believed was a reflection of iconoclastic freedom—that of nonconformity, personal choice, and pluralistic self-expression—was a catastrophic choice. In perhaps his most famous song, "Nuclear War," released in 1982, amid concerns of a possible nuclear holocaust between the United States and the Soviet Union, Ra implored listeners to recognize that nuclear war was a brutal possibility. Mutilation, disfigurement, and destruction required nothing more than a push of the button. As the song went, "nuclear war / nuclear war / they talkin' about / nuclear war . . . it's a motherfucker, don't you know . . . if they push that button, your ass must go . . . they'll blast you so high in the sky . . . you'll kiss your ass goodbye . . . radiation . . . mutation . . . fire . . . hydrogen bombs . . . atomic bombs . . . what you gonna do without yo ass?"[13] Ra was no Luddite. This was obvious given his interest in experimenting with cutting-edge sound technologies and his faith in the redemptive possibilities of outer-space exploration. But his belief was that technology without any moral consciousness became disastrous because it had no center through which to regulate itself. "Nuclear War" drew a parallel between the fantasy of American nuclear deterrence based on mutually assured destruction—a notion based on the hyperrationality of rational choice and game theory—and a dangerous American cultural optimism that such a thing could never happen. The Arkestra's prophetic punctuated chorus of interruptive "yeahs" throughout the song served as a counterpoint to a depoliticized citizen who wished to reach the afterlife rather than engage the exigencies of the present. Ra tried to shake people from their moral slumber: Wake up! Nuclear holocaust could easily happen!

But Ra's address across the racial line was augmented by a specific one to the white majority too invested in its dream of invulnerability to recognize its moral apathy. He eschewed traditional political proposals for redress, but he declared greater social consciousness was nonnegotiable during "perilous times," for if white citizens "chose" to "ignore that warning," the future would be much like the past.[14] The closest analogue to Ra's cultural criticism was found in the existential graffiti-paintings of one of his younger contemporaries, Jean-Michel Basquiat. Both agreed American culture's promise of abundance and undisturbed middle-class family life distorted human freedom, while leaving in place the apathy that brings people of color closer to death.[15] Ra's abstract expressionist poetry was not unlike Basquiat's *Untitled* (1987), in which minimalistic drawings of everyday objects like hatchets, cats, ducks, rakes, rye, and oat are sprawled on his canvas and squeezed alongside vicious dogs, jail, and an electric fence and phrases like "nothing to be gained here." For both, American desires of security and anonymity had devastating social costs. Basquiat's and Ra's work countered the idea being circulated in the postwar period under the rubric of the liberal consensus in texts like Swedish social scientist Gunnar Myrdal's *The American Dilemma* (1944), which argued that racial equality would come from black cultural assimilation into the mainstream.[16] For Ra and Basquiat, unlike Myrdal, what needed to happen instead was that black and white people needed to collectively reconstruct America, what Ra called a "mean world."

Part of the reason Ra's message was at times so difficult to hear had to do with the way it was framed. His prophetic vision bordered on the messianic in ways that alienated secularists, humanists, and radical skeptics. And Ra's paternalistic leadership over his Arkestra stood in stark opposition to the transformative potential of the collaborative dialectical art displayed in its improvised performances. Though the band had women members throughout its existence, both men and women were expected to adhere to specific diets, remain sober, live celibate lifestyles and have little material wealth. Ra's approach stemmed from his faith in elite rule, which was displayed in the experimental science fiction film that he wrote and starred in, *Space Is the Place* (1974). The narrative centered on Ra's return to Oakland after space traveling to a different planet for black relocation only to leave prematurely because of a conspiratorial collusion led by the FBI and the black "overseer," who wants to profit from black suffering in the United States. This was a Platonic ideal of leadership found in Ra's self-presentation as a black savior who journeyed to a distant land to find truth only to be subverted by the interests of established corrupt modes of power. Though *Space Is the Place* productively exposed the way ideas of masculine "black power" from the 1960s that were invested in American ideals did not guarantee liberation, Ra would controversially say that he preferred "weakness" to "power."[17]

FREEDOM AND FUTURE

And yet, Ra's elitism always stood in contrast with his attempt to espouse a capacious notion of freedom unbound to singular expectations. It is true that Ra refused to engage in the classical political-theoretical debate about whether freedom was the absence of external constraints or something about the good life.

And at times, he often seemed to reject the idea altogether, sounding like a conservative when he prioritized "precision" and "discipline."[18] But closer inspection reveals that Ra favored a definition of freedom based on self-expression and autonomy within a community and the idea of democratic individualism. His poem "Unseen Definitions" (1980) gave value to this constructive, deconstructive, dialectical vision, in which freedom's emptiness—it could be an "empty shell"—without human elaboration could lead to new visions, but also conceal unequal power structures and meanings—"unseen definitions"—and quickly become a "trigger word of tragic illusion."[19] In this sense, his critique of freedom as an "illusion" was centered on its narrowly liberal formulations, which stressed personal choice, nonintervention and rugged individualism. In contrast, his idea of freedom was defined by elaboration by its practitioners and awareness of its tragic failures. Freedom would need to be refreshed and reimagined.

This was a jazz-like improvisational notion of freedom, as a mixing and matching of competing ideals and visions, which was found in Ra's music. And it was his music that he thought could be a model for politics. Collaboration between instruments and musicians provided a network of support not only during moments of failure—a missed note here or there. But it together created something better tested and reworked. Instruments could sound out of tune when they were played individually, Ra insisted, but a new sound emerged when they played in tandem, opening up new sounds and emotional experiences that reorganized understandings about their function and sound.[20] It is within this context that Ra's recurrent talk of what he called "natural difference" and his critique of equality should be properly understood. Not as a reactionary assault on equal human dignity or basic resources to sustain life. But as an existential and ontological claim about the inescapabilty of pluralism—different chords, sounds, possibilities, and creative acts.[21]

For Ra, realizing human pluralism required not a narrowing of individualism, but a complete reevaluation and broadening of obligation. In contrast to what he saw as "a poor world, poor in spiritual values, void of natural contact with the natural infinity/otherness being," he wanted a world in which violence was replaced with cosmic love, self-interest with a sense of responsibility for all of humanity.[22] This was expressed through his short-lived nonprofit organization, "Ihnfinity Inc.," started with his business manager, Alton Abraham, in Chicago in 1967, which had a global orientation. Strikingly, it was formed at the very moment when the black radicalism of the Black Panther Party and SNCC (Student National Coordinating Committee) seemed like the only radical alternative to integrationist liberalism. In contrast to this position, Ra and Abraham defended neither black self-defense nor greater civic involvement, but the idea that all humanity should have a share of the universe. Ra would perform works of a "humanitarian nature among all people of the earth," to encourage people to live creatively, to do research, to have access to land, shelter, and water, and to control the means of production.[23]

The Arkestra's jazz compositions further testified sonically to what Ra tried to embody in his performances and persona. This was a free blackness that could not be disciplined or determined by convention. What one hears is a piercing cymbal, a vibrant trumpet, or electronic sounds that sound like Morse code clicks that, through their methodical repetition and increasing frequency and speed, conjure the arrival of a new emotional and intellectual space. Eerie echoes of a distant-sounding keyboard are juxtaposed against barely audible chants that call forth a semiwaking state, which is as opaque as it is open for exploration. The Arkestra's futuristic sounds, coupled with Ra's insistence on black space exploration, reconstituted ideas about black belongingness that exceeded existing binaries of citizenship—between American and African, individualist and Pan-African.

Granting black citizens the presumptive authority to be space travelers was, for Ra, never about the project of colonization or Americanization. It was connected to unconditional generosity and critical respect. This was evident in his paeans to black people, social outcasts, and experimental thinkers and in his own composition process and live performances. In his poem "Message To Black Youth" (1971), the speaker named unloved and disregarded black youth as loved and as not needing to prove their humanity.[24] As he put it in "My Music Is Words," "Even the least of brothers has his day and when you realize the meaning of that day, you will feel the presence of an angel in disguise."[25] Ra thus reconstituted individualism away from its most narrow self-interested formulation. He made it about radical self-examination and truth-telling like James Baldwin in *The Fire Next Time* (1963). But Ra's love was much more cosmic than Baldwin's. Ra's "Other Gods Have I Heard Of" (1972) updated the American poet Walt Whitman's love letter to humanity and his naming of all that was considered marginal in *Leaves of Grass* (1855). Ra collapsed hierarchies of value between deities and ordinary people. He positioned love as a force that was beyond economic calculation and rationalization, when he said, "And the Greater love has no god than I / For I like my greater love / Am Immeasurable."[26] Furthermore, Ra's "The Other Otherness" (1972) rendered greater knowledge as antithetical to the claim of sovereignty and power. It did this while making communication not about mastery, but about relinquishing the fantasy of control, for "When one understands / There is no ego involved / There is no communication / in the supervised state of distances."[27] The fundamental meaning behind Ra's idea of freedom as "the freedom to rise above a cruel planet" was about transcending an unequal, dehumanizing world order that placed profit above humanity and social control over untapped democratic possibility.

For Ra, art could become a transformative social antidote. Not simply because politics was too corrupted by power and narrowly concerned with strategy, but because culture's preoccupation with creative expression could create visions of the future from which to rethink the present. Although Ra never consistently defended nonviolence with much philosophical rigor, he tried to sever the connection between violence and politics. Like earlier modernists associated with the avant-garde—abstract expressionists, cubists, and futurists—making art into a weapon politicized its function. And it switched weaponization away from the stage of armed conflict into the realm of aesthetics. In 1974, after giving a concert in Central Park in New York City with a hundred-person musician band, he expressed his desire for something much more epic: a collection of ten thousand musicians—the number later became 144,000—to perform a sacred concert that could "melt all the atomic bombs" and make the world peaceful.[28] The theoretical justification for this was expressed in his poem "Points of the Space Age," which linked culture to a new barometer for a new humanity by saying, "A nation without art is a nation without a lifeline. / Art is the lifeline because art is the airy concept / Of greater living."[29] These words summarized Ra's primary philosophical objective: to sanctify the ephemeral and subjective conditions of creativity, while severing collective life from the goal of ruthless industrialization, automated efficiency maximization, lifeless bureaucracy, and mindless competition.

UTOPIAN ICONOCLASM

Ra's poetic message—much like his musical compositions—was less philosophically clear and more improvisational and shrouded in mystery than his utopian predecessors. But it was much more fully embodied in his life. Ra tried to live out the utopian aesthetic that was only outlined in literature. In fact, he tried to make his life literary. Precisely because of this, although it is impossible to reduce Ra's utopian individualism to any concrete political ideology, it allows one to think more clearly about dominant expressions of the political. Ra's ideas were never going to be operationalized. No one thought outer space was really the answer. But his thoughts probed questions about the ethics and necessity of what was central to the twentieth century: capitalist inequality, ongoing war, white supremacy, de jure and de facto racial segregation, and black ghettoization.

At the same time, Ra's embodiment of utopia provided its most spirited defense of its possibility and gave the most ammunition for its greatest critics. This was at precisely the moment when utopia was being discredited, abandoned, and described as only responsible for totalitarian fascism and communism. On stage and in public, Ra was always more of a myth than Herman Blount. But he was a myth that performed contradiction, inspired hope, gave joy, and induced frustration and confusion to stimulate something new and fresh in his audience. Something they didn't think was ever possible.

7

SAMUEL DELANY AND THE AMBIGUITY OF UTOPIA

By the time the black novelist Samuel R. Delany (1942–) wrote his science fiction work *Trouble on Triton: An Ambiguous Heterotopia* (1976), black utopian political visions were all but evaporated. The postwar dream of Pan-Africanism seemed less likely than ever before. This was the case especially after the coup d'état of Nkrumah in Ghana in 1966, the rise of mass bureaucratization, political authoritarianism, and economic corruption throughout the globe. The end of Stalinist totalitarianism in the early 1950s created a version of Soviet Communism in the 1970s based on stagnation and cynicism that offered no alternative to Western capitalist inequality. Malcolm's dream after 1964 of anti-imperialist social democracy worldwide was left unfulfilled. Black rebellions in response to police brutality and socioeconomic inequality throughout major US cities only intensified white backlash. The legislative gains of the civil rights movement came under assault by an ascendant new right orthodoxy. This conservative coalition offered law and order and traditional family values in the place of political rights and socioeconomic freedom. History moves in ebbs and flows. If the 1960s generated a sense of profound optimism for radical social transformation, the 1970s witnessed the resurgence of reaction.

By proposing an alternative vision to this political milieu, Delany refused the temptation of escapism.[1] As a direct literary

FIGURE 7.1 Samuel R. Delany. Photograph by Alex Lozupone. https://commons.wikimedia.org/wiki/File:Loz_delany_2015.png.

response to Ursula Le Guin's science fiction novel *The Dispossessed: An Ambiguous Utopia* (1974), *Triton* defended the novel's anarchist utopia and its rejection of capitalist patriarchy, but replaced its narrative of romantic resolution with one of paradox.[2] Complex neologisms, fast-paced narrative shifts, and futuristic technological inventions made *Triton* a best seller, which sold almost one million copies. But this did not diminish its theoretical imagination. Delany understood the critical scorn often attributed to the so-called marginal literature of science fiction. It was deemed not to be rigorous, sacrificing artistic complexity for mass appeal. But by excavating the lives of marginal identities—gender nonconformists, people of color, and women—in a futuristic society, *Triton* provincialized the meaning of the universal and broadened political theory for the oppressed. As he said, "To write clearly, accurately, with knowledge of and respect for the marginal is to be controversial—especially if you're honest about the overlaps. Because that means it's harder to regard the marginal as 'other.' And at that point, the whole category system that has assigned values like central and marginal in the first place is threatened."[3] In fact, Delany saw the task of science fiction writers much like that of historians. Whereas the historian resists the logic of turning the past into something that is profitable for the present, the science fiction writer brings into a relief a future that is not driven by the demands of the present, but explodes its common sense.[4]

Triton's immediate literary inheritance was the dystopian fiction of George Orwell, Philip K. Dick, and Aldous Huxley that decried social conformity, technological rationality, depersonalized bureaucracy, and mass society. But its political critique was not based on the liberalism of equal political rights, individual freedom, and plurality. *Triton* was instead a pioneering text for what would later be known as "queer theory," but its radicalism came from its attempt to fuse African American literature with a critique of power. It did this through blending Frankfurt School critical theory, feminist critique, and French poststructuralism. These were the intellectual movements that Delany was influenced by as a writer working in the academy in the 1960s and 1970s. What made *Triton* remarkable was this: few literary texts before or since have been able to combine and politicize such eclectic traditions, all while meditating on utopia. *Triton*'s futuristic romantic arc set in 2112 told the story of

Bron Helstrom, a white male former sex-worker, who becomes jaded about social liberation and experiences unrequited love. The novel was ultimately an antiutopian narrative of frustrated self-consciousness, of a problematic freedom in a world where desire seemed limitlessly realizable and in a pluralistic society where social identities could be made, remade, and unmade.

Delany's antiutopianism came from his view that utopia presupposed a "static, unchanging, and rather tyrannical world."[5] Yet, this idea was both realized in *Triton's* narrative and betrayed by its articulation of a spirit of utopia. The novel defended an ethos of citizenship that appreciated ambiguity without permanent resolution instead of codified social norms. *Triton*'s subtitle, "An Ambiguous Heterotopia," was revealed through the way social freedom facilitates radical experiments in desire, self-making, and community. But they are also manipulated by reactionary forces for repressive ends. *Triton* imagined the "hetero-topia" as the other space of utopia/dystopia. It gave rise to a futuristic emancipatory queer politics while warning of the way it could smuggle in destructive patriarchy, misogynistic violence, and political authoritarianism.

Delany's avowed poststructuralist philosophy distinguished him from earlier black utopians. He believed that the incommensurable space between language's power to name and absolute truth "created the field on which" the market, the state, "as well as the more blatant processes of external corruption, internal distortion, and media manipulation . . . can wreak their political violences."[6] But Delany's postructuralist ethical mantra broadly resonated with the utopian tradition. This was the idea that subjecting power to immanent critique would forge a society in which freedom became more of a reality for most. And it would create a world where what seemed fixed became overturned. In this way, Delany's preoccupation with deconstruction paralleled

Du Bois's in "The Comet," but it shared the hallmarks of the black utopian dramatization of what power wanted to hide in order to reveal what was hidden within its crevices and unseen vulnerabilities.

More broadly, *Triton* pushed the black utopian tradition to consider intersections of race, gender, and sexuality just as it unsettled expectations about them. Delany's idea of utopia was arguably more countercultural than those before it. It exploded extant binaries, desanctified social conventions, and rendered respectability morally bankrupt. *Triton* exposed utopia's dystopian undertones more fully than utopian and antiutopian texts before it. It did so with philosophical rigor that exceeded Schuyler's fiction from the 1930s and raised the stakes for utopia's staunchest defenders.

QUEER IDENTIFICATIONS AND DISORIENTING THE POLITICAL

Triton's world founded in boundless freedom does not create chaos and disorder. In doing so it counters heteronormative sexuality and the patriarchal nuclear family depicted as enlivening by the new right. *Triton* secularized and gave political form to the unconventional family structures expressed through the nineteenth-century Oneida colonies. And it imagined as uncontroversial the most radical arguments of the women's and gay liberation movements in the 1960s. Free love, self-expression, and desire trumped the demands of social reproduction. In Triton, marriage and sex-work is illegal, gender fluidity is encouraged, and sexual preference is shifting because it could be what the novel called "refixed." The general notion of family is flexible through the many gender plural and nonconforming co-ops in which citizens could live. *Triton*'s nonbinary, queer-positive society resists moral puritanism and heterosexual respectability. Freedom could be free from what Freud saw as the Victorian morality that repressed the drives of Eros (love) and Thanatos (death). In a sense, *Triton* extended Herbert Marcuse's view in *Eros and Civilization* (1956): unbridled pleasure would lead not to social disorder, but to new forms of cooperation. This was realized through *Triton*'s organizing metaphor of the anarchic unlicensed ("u-l") sector. Its lawlessness doesn't create more crime, but created unwritten laws that come from the demands of collective life.[7]

By problematizing Freud's heteronormative Oedipal theory of illicit desire, Delany described queer identification as creating unexpected solidarities. Lawrence, one of Bron's older roommates, self-identifies as a "political homosexual" and says, "The true mark of social intelligence is how unusual we can make our particular behavior."[8] Delany undermined expectations about political identification and exposed as morally questionable the wish to transform sexual desire into a political statement. This is unnecessary when gender is socially fluid and severed from heterosexual norms. Nowhere is this clearer than in the critical interrogation of Lawrence's queer identification by the leader of a theater troupe and Bron's love interest, "The Spike." She says, "he can have his sexuality refixed on someone, or thing, that can get it up for him. . . . Sexual point-proving is such a waste of time."[9]

Triton's critique of social liberation extended to instrumental rationality. Triton's information-driven society dependent upon mapping out human relationships for the sake of progress is co-opted by arbitrary political power. State-sponsored social programs in communal living create a mass surveillance society that squashes civic dissent.[10] *Triton* further identified the exclusionary thrust of the positivism, which systematized truth as a set of logical maximums but made it devoid of moral consideration. This is illustrated through what *Triton* called "metalogics."[11] Metalogics were Delany's commentary on the ways in which the dream of scientific mastery is a nightmare because purely logical reasoning gives validity to the fiction of a coherent identity. This requires no scrutiny and sidesteps questions of ethical citizenship. As the doctor who performs Bron's gender reassignment surgery says, "with life enclosed between two vast parenthesis of nonbeing and striated on either side by inevitable suffering, there is no logical reason ever to try to improve any situation."[12]

Naturalizing the logical binaries of "metalogics" without considering their hierarchical nature keeps intact intersectional oppression. Bron is shocked to hear that a black coworker, Miriamne, accuses him of arbitrary power for sexually harassing and firing her. And Bron's meandering explanation of metalogics to Miriamne through the hue of whiteness as the logical antithesis of blackness evacuates the sociohistorical context necessary to address domination. Delany understood race not simply as a socially constructed reality, but as a "biological fantasy," structured around specific institutions of "political oppression."[13] This is why Triton's status as a postracial society, dramatized by the ways in which "nigger" is freely floated around without specific connotations to black people and without derogatory intent, is betrayed by Bron's racist reduction of Miriamne's expression of her unique black family history as dating back to Kenya to her cultural identity of lawlessness. As Bron tells her, "typical u-l . . . always talking about where they came from, where their families started."[14] The oppressive link between logical binaries, instrumental objectification, and objectifying male desire is further displayed through Bron's anger toward Spike's repeated romantic refusal. This is summarized through Lawrence's critique of his behavior: "She simply doesn't exist," he tells Bron, "I mean how can she? You're a logical sadist looking for a logical masochist."[15]

SUBVERSIVE FREEDOM AND ITS SUBVERSION

But *Triton*'s central critique of utopianism centered on freedom. Delany intervened in a post-1960s moment when a brief expansion of social power for the most marginalized American citizens—women, queer, black, disabled—fostered resentment from the dominant class. Bron was Delany's metaphor for white citizens in the post–civil rights era struggling to cope with feelings of social diminishment. *Triton* presented white male heterosexual perceptions of victimhood as distortions of social reality. Although it took seriously Bron's existential crisis, it also exposed as dangerous his resentment of self-making in a world without established power. As Bron puts it, "But what happens to those of us who don't know? . . . who have problems and don't know why we have the problems we do? . . . [have] lost . . . all connection with articulate reason. Decide what you like and go get it? Well, what about the ones of us who know what we don't like?"[16]

Bron is incapable of articulating his desire, to know what he wants, to realize his own vision of the good. This constitutes the dialectic between the beauty and the limits of utopian pluralism. On the one hand, as a poststructuralist influenced by the psychoanalyst Jacques Lacan's theory of desire, which was always mediated by language, Delany resisted naturalized accounts of freedom. As Delany explained, "The mutual inadequations of language and desire constitute what happens; the mutual inadequations of desire and what happens constitute language; the mutual inadequations of what happens and language constitute desire."[17] From Delany's vantage point, Bron is right. There is, in fact, no such thing as pure desire. Everything is part of a discourse, a set of words. Life is located within this gap of incommensurability, rather than on either of its poles. On the other hand, Bron is wrong to believe that what desire signifies and who is socially allowed to pursue freedom is free from hierarchy. The history of white supremacy and patriarchy are formative in this regard.

If anything, *Triton*'s thesis was that citizens who yearned for the comforts of home would populate utopia. This would be the case even if home were only welcoming to an exclusive few. The political legitimacy for all citizens to partake in the freedom of critical dissent and nonconformity initially designed for the marginalized would be co-opted by reactionary forces. Bron's psychological vulnerability and thirst for power overshadow the social value of expanding freedom to the most vulnerable. [18]

In this way, Bron's gender-reassignment surgery from man to woman is both a creative act of self-reimagination and a culmination of masculine domination. The biological male sexual supremacy overturned through Bron's embrace of female sexuality does not overturn her gendered worldview of masculine virility and feminine docility. As Bron says, "Sometimes I wish men were all strong and women were all weak . . . because, somehow, it would be simpler that way to justify."[19] Suggesting that manhood could be reconstructed was Delany's feminist dream. But understanding how womanhood could smuggle in patriarchy to justify traditional gender roles was his realistic assessment. Outlining limitless opportunities of self-invention was Delany's defense of performativity. But his concern was that this would intensify the spirit of competition and asocial individualism. Lawrence is startled by Bron's inability to appreciate that "women have been treated like human beings only the last sixty five years . . . and are less willing to put up with certain kinds of shit than men." In response to such criticism Bron says, "We need that particularly male aloneness . . . if only for the ingenuity it breeds, so that the rest of the species can survive."[20]

Bron was *Triton*'s metaphor for the citizen that embodied an authoritarian antidemocratic state. She internalizes a repressive attitude and is unwilling to transform identity into a countercultural counterweight. Bron fictionalized Delany's worries in the 1970s. As Delany said, as "the women's movement and the gay rights movement have gotten away from the civil rights movement as model, both have found themselves backsliding into far more reactionary positions than, at former times, they once dared to occupy. . . . Since material changes didn't arrive to stabilize some of the answers, those answers simply couldn't be held onto."[21] The sense of idealism became conservative realism. The dream of sexual plurality and nonconformity became narrowly defined through a set of false choices—"respectable" or "nonrespectable." Liberation became incremental progress.

Yet what is lost for Bron was *Triton*'s articulation of the spirit of utopia in which freedom needs to embody a state of becoming. Impossible is it to have complete knowledge about what the future would bring. This philosophy is concretized through Sam, a black transgender man. As a government worker, he shifts from a true believer into a radical skeptic after both he and Bron are tortured on Earth. And he transforms this shift into a maxim: "the only advice I can give you is that even if it's hard where you are now—and I know it can be—you're still changing, still moving. Eventually, even from here, you'll get somewhere else."[22] Though the narrative was based on exposing the tyrannical dimensions of perfection, *Triton* extended the black utopian argument that transformative energy could be mined from the ashes of failure. *Triton* hoped readers would accept what Bron briefly glimpsed after Triton's government exterminates three-quarters of Earth's population to conclude its interplanetary war: the productive power of fallibility, of living between the boundaries and borders, rather than trying to codify them.

POSTSTRUCTURAL ETHICS

In *Triton*'s estimate, living in this precarious condition requires a transformed notion of love. Delany rejected the idea of love as pure romantic connection because it masked its foundation in a capitalist exchange logic, where anything could be bought or sold. As Delany once put it, "You can't be friends with—or certainly not love—someone you buy something from. . . . In this case, love/desire is hypostatized as the originary, metaphysical absolute to which any material exchange is always inadequate."[23] Spike recognizes the theoretically generative nature of her ex-lover's rejection and forgiveness of her wish for violent intimacy with him: "he calls me one of the people he *loves*. . . . If you *really* love someone . . . you'll *do* that. *Even* that."[24] This was just one example of the way *Triton* excavated the unconditional acceptance of loss from the fantasy of possession. Spike calls out the latent will to power in Lawrence's identification with political homosexuality. Lawrence critiques Bron's masculinism within his newfound womanhood. Miriamne denounces Bron's colorblind racism. And Sam rejects Bron's wish for control. Love is revised from a simple act into a set of choices defined by an ethos of truth-telling. It requires as much elaboration as the shifting boundaries of intimacy upon which it depends. Transformed in *Triton* as ethically valuable was not resolution, but the vulnerability that came from the moment when reconciliation seemed impossible, after all seemed lost, if not irrevocably violated.

Triton's overarching message was that absolute certainty needed to be sacrificed for ambiguity. Necessary is it to reject the binaries that create what the German philosopher Carl Schmitt once defined as "the political"—the creation of "friends and enemies" defined by incommensurable existential divisions. *Triton*'s anti-Schmittian sensibility is captured through Bron's last words after the conclusion of Triton's war. She expresses ambivalence about the dividing line between truth and falsehood and feels distressed about a range of prior commitments: the value of political freedom, the necessity of war, nationalism, and national security. She moves back and forth, from certainty to skepticism:

> You can see, both back and ahead, the morass where truth and falsity are simply, for you, indistinguishable. . . . Here I am, on Triton, and again I am lost in some hopeless tangle of confusion, trouble, and distress. But this so silly! . . . suddenly and shockingly! . . . she was sure . . . the subjective was held politically inviolable; and hadn't they just killed three out of four, or five out of six, to keep it so—? Then, as suddenly, sureness ceased. . . . But . . . no, not if she had felt like that about it . . . it sure would never come.[25]

Delany transformed poststructural critique into an ethical project. *Triton* made the task for those concerned with liberation more speculative and deconstructive, more imaginative and self-critical. What is necessary is to retain the spirit of utopia—of love, justice, freedom—as a horizon that could never be fully attained. But also to balance it with vigilance about it being infiltrated by power—being ossified and imprisoned by its own idealism and openness. Living simultaneously between these two worlds is precarious. This is because it threatens to empty engaged citizenship from the critical rationality necessary to engage in a systematic critique of total domination. Delany's hope was that this would not be the case. That critical vigilance would preclude this from happening.

Triton didn't offer concrete solutions, but its deconstructive method is still applicable today. Much has changed since *Triton* was published in the 1970s, especially debates about sexual liberation. American attitudes about gender and sexuality have become increasingly liberalized. And conversations that would have seemed unimaginable even a decade ago—trans-people's rights, gender nonconformity, sexuality existing on a spectrum and irreducible to binary opposition—have become part of public discourse. But as *Triton* prophesized, changing perceptions mean little without dismantling power. And power is as durable as ever. Some combination of sexual violence, domestic abuse, rape, and pay disparity structures the lives of most American women. Trans-people are murdered at exceedingly high rates, while queer men and women—though embraced within American institutions of national security like the military—continue to suffer homophobic dehumanization in all realms of life. From *Triton,* we learn that the task is to live on and between the margins of ethics and critique. It is to preclude power from monopolizing the spirit of utopia while demonstrating how that spirit threatens to be codified by it.

8

OCTAVIA BUTLER AND THE POLITICS OF UTOPIAN TRANSCENDENCE

The black science fiction writer Octavia E. Butler (1947–2006) published her two dystopian books, *Parable of the Sower* (1993) and *Parable of the Talents* (1998), when utopian dreams of racial justice were stillborn. Leftist intellectuals proclaimed the end of the twentieth-century dream of economic equality and dignity for all. With the collapse of democratic socialism and the hegemonic triumph of liberal capitalism, lost were the enlightenment universalism and aspiration for radical democracy. This is what Francis Fukuyama famously called "the end of history."[1] At the time, Butler was best known for her dystopian neoslave narrative of time travel, *Kindred* (1979), which earned her the reputation as one of the great American fantasy writers. The book was more fact than fiction as an account of American racism. The story centered upon the trope of time travel—the return of a black woman from the 1970s to an antebellum plantation to keep alive a young boy who would become the slave master to initiate her family bloodline. As a historical revision meant to trouble its moment's postracialism, *Kindred* upended vaunted American liberal consensus narratives of racial progress and equality that were booming in the post–civil rights era.

FIGURE 8.1 Octavia E. Butler. Photograph by Nikolas Coukouma. https://commons.wikimedia.org/wiki/File:Butler_signing.jpg.

But the *Parable* books were less works of magical realism and more prophetic critique of what American culture was and where it was headed. Just as *Parable* implicated American capitalist liberal democracy in creating a future dystopian social disaster it denied, it simultaneously vaulted Butler into the American cultural mainstream. She won the Nebula and Hugo awards for science fiction writing and earned the prestigious MacArthur genius fellowship in 1995. Set in postapocalyptic Los Angeles, where Butler was born and lived most her life, in 2024 and 2032, the *Parable* series was an unflinching reversal of American investments in freedom, political order, and moral virtue. It did this through a first-person narrative of a hero whose perspective had usually been disauthorized and denigrated from American literature generally. A young black woman, Lauren Oya Olamina, builds a multiracial intentional community called "Acorn," which is based on a countercultural movement called "Earthseed." She does this amid threats from the totalitarian Christian Right, which assumes power as a response to widespread economic inequality.

Butler's lifelong pessimism about the human condition informed her fiction. *Parable* was nothing short of a horrific narrative about the neoliberal platform of free markets, economic deregulation, the erosion of the social welfare state, "tough on crime" policies, and the Christian Right's antireproductive rights commitment and wish to fuse church and state. But *Parable* was also a work of futuristic vision. Although it followed *Triton*'s refusal to center its narrative exclusively on race, by being the first science fiction work to cast a black woman as its central protagonist, it deconstructed the whiteness of science fiction. Butler's politics were never clear. Her skepticism of civil rights liberal integrationism and Black Power racial separatism made *Parable* eschew traditional questions of political strategy. This is perhaps why most of the critical literature has emphasized Butler's radical aesthetic and significant cultural achievements rather than politics. For instance, her attempt to reclaim an Afrocentric narrative of history, to bring forth what Ralph Ellison called its "boomerang"[2] and to undo binaries of the modern and traditional, sacred and profane, high and low culture.[3] But less appreciated is that *Parable* was a work of political theory. Its rejection of neoliberal and Christian utopianism coexisted with a defense of a black democratic counterpoint serviceable for critique and resistance.

Butler took black utopia into a more dystopian direction than ever before, but also in a more feminist one. She treated utopia with the same deconstructive spirit as Delany but dramatized a clear ethical and moral vision not seen since Du Bois and Ra. Her critique of utopia was based less on Schuyler's cynicism or Delany's academic rigor and more on a tragicomic faith that something better, more enlivening could emerge from the ashes of disaster. This optimistic hope for future democracy that Butler expressed with more urgency and frequency late in life was apparent. It gave texture to *Parable*'s spirit of utopia and outlined the ease with which it could be co-opted in ways that deactivated its radical potential. [4]

AMERICAN UTOPIAS, NEOLIBERAL NIGHTMARES

Butler rejected the neoliberal dreams of privatization announced in the 1990s as the alternative to the social welfare state. In *Parable*, economic freedom leads not to greater personal choice, but to its opposite: greater violence and insecurity. The glamorization of entrepreneurialism is the cause for ongoing global war over limited resources. The free markets seen by libertarians as protecting against political tyranny create human catastrophe. The evisceration of government creates an eviscerated life, which reregulates itself through the deprivation it experiences. Unregulated industries create global warming. Rising sea levels devastate neighborhoods. School privatization creates massive inequities in learning opportunities. Arsonists who don't have jobs get erotic pleasure from burning neighborhoods to the ground by using a profitable designer psychopharmacological drug, "pyro."

This creates a dangerous redistribution of power. Modern political thought long held that sovereignty over punishment was reserved for an ostensibly neutral state uninterested in profit maximization. But unbridled privatization transfers this power to security forces protecting segregated middle-class neighborhoods and homogenous suburbs, whose rationale for existence is to serve the particular interests that pay them. It creates the very reality it aims to combat: the homeless populations suffering from mental illness, addiction, and poverty.

The instrumental thinking behind such market solutions to political order creates a dangerous kind of what the French philosopher Michel Foucault called "biopolitical" economy. In *Parable of the Sower*, President Christopher Donner calls for getting people back to work, but in a way that is empty of adequate consideration of the quality of their lives or socioeconomic resources—decent living spaces, healthcare, and childcare.[5] As Olamina says,

> Donner has a plan for putting people back to work. . . . What's adequate, I wonder: A house or apartment? A room? A bed in a shared in room? A barracks bed? Space on a floor? Space on the ground? And what about people with big families? Won't they be seen as bad investments? . . . Will it be legal to poison, mutilate, or infect people—as long as you provide them with food, water and space to die?[6]

Placing profit above humans makes socially vulnerable populations unfortunate remainders, if not the dispensable excess, of a community. Here, Butler indicted technological rationality and scientific progress: Drugs like "parateco" maximized learning acquisition but have deadly side effects like the death of Olamina's mother during childbirth. And "slave collars," meant to be efficient modes of punishment, become the primary tool for sex-trafficking, slave labor, and child abuse.

A biopolitical society engenders a vicious cycle of fear and resentment. This incapacitates a critical civil society. Strikingly, this is never directed from a clear power structure from above, but is actually internalized from below. Olamina harbors suspicion toward young children living within the shadows of the demolished and abandoned streets. She suspects them of theft, murder, and rape: "I think if there were only one or two us, or if they couldn't see our guns, they might try to pull us down and steal our bikes, our clothes. . . . Then what? Rape? Murder?"[7] *Parable* thus objected to explanations of the erosion of civic society that centered on hyperindividualism emergent from generational cultural-change shifts. Instead, the cause is systemic socioeconomic deprivation.[8] Solidarity is eliminated through the erosion of the very idea of collective life. There is no public space of the commons. Social precariousness makes distrust contagious when government obligation is detached from underlying systemic conditions, when housing is delinked from improved mental health and when nourishment is separated from a healthier body politic.

But state power became especially effective at total domination through controlling discourse. The emancipatory potential of language dramatized by earlier black utopians was given an Orwellian take in *Parable*. In the two books, language divides, conquers, disciplines, and enforces docility. Citizens are reclassified as "vagrants" for the purpose of resettling their children with so-called respectable families. And after Earthseed's colony, Acorn, is captured by the government, it is renamed "Camp Christian." And Olamina and her followers refer to their captors as "teachers," and are forced to sing, testify, and pray. Christian America's very desire for linguistic conformity dramatized what totalitarian power wants to accomplish—creating boundaries of social difference and hierarchies of moral value.

What *Triton* found in social pluralism, *Parable* found in religious fundamentalism fused with neoliberalism: political hopelessness that created nostalgic dreams to reestablish systems of domination that never worked for the oppressed.[9] "Our adults haven't been wiped out by a plague so they're still anchored in the past," Olamina says, "waiting for the good old days to come back."[10] Collective despair creates fantasies of patriarchal dominance and traditional nuclear families, which threaten women's liberation. *Parable*'s male characters are obsessed with single-handedly protecting their families and politicians across the ideological spectrum promise "a return . . . to glory, wealth, and order."[11]

In this way, *Parable* fictionalized Marx's theory of capitalist ideological inversion. Economically constructed inequities, productive of arbitrary elite power, appear natural and thus alienate citizens from their popular power, while making obedience natural. The rise of Senator Andre Steele Jarret and his religious fundamentalist movement in *Parable of the Talents* exposed how religious fundamentalist utopia depoliticized and moralized human disaster, which was created through human choices of free-market capitalism. As Jarret asks, "Are we Christian? Are we? . . . We are God's people, or we are filth? We are God's people, or we are nothing!"[12] Under conditions of distress, salvation is seen as possible only through deference to orthodoxy. This is true for most, but especially for the most vulnerable, whose very survival depends upon a community. These were the poor, who work "dangerous, dirty jobs," and "women who are abused," "want to be fooled, need to be fooled."[13]

PARADOXES OF TRANSCENDENCE AND RESISTANCE

Butler countered this American dystopia with Olamina's philosophy of Earthseed. But she simultaneously questioned its transformative political potential. Earthseed blends ideas of Christian redemption, New Age ecoconsciousness, and secular transcendental humanism. Its overarching idea is that "God is Change." In opposition to the rigidity enforced by the security state, Earthseed found freedom within "adaptability and persistent, positive obsession." "Without adaptability," so declares a line from the book Olamina authors and disseminates to her followers as gospel, *Earthseed: Books of the Living*, "what remains may be channeled into destructive fanaticism. Without positive obsession, there is nothing at all."[14] Earthseed is represented as a philosophy of immanence, of living from within—rather than trying to escape—the world's boundaries, of coping with and adapting to what occurs. Earthseed defines community as something made through free decisions and commitments, rather than a preexisting entity that one is born into or to which one naturally belonged. The bonds of attachment create its boundaries, but those boundaries are elastic and shifting because its existence depends on action: "We have our island community, fragile, and yet a fortress. Sometimes it seems too small and weak to survive . . . It persists. We persist. This is our place, no matter what."[15]

Parable defended Earthseed as a revolutionary philosophy of resilience capable of building a democratic future. But at virtually every turn throughout both books, it complicated this hope, exploring the way it could become a depoliticized form of escapism that eschewed collective struggle against existing power structures. Without question, Butler's attempt to strip Earthseed of exclusionary fundamentalist theological overtones and her presentation of it as progressive religion stemmed from her religious agnosticism. But *Parable* depicted Earthseed as an example of how religious asceticism basked in resentment and moral superiority keeps domination intact.[16] The transcendent energy of hoping for a better future gives Acorn the energy to resist their enslavement at the hands of Christian Crusaders in *Parable of the Talents*. But it is transformed into something of a protectionist isolationist nation-state. In times of both crisis and relative peace, Acorn concentrates its efforts inward at organizational perpetuation and exclusively focuses attention on the missionary work of converting future recruits and colonizing outer space.

Parable valued Earthseed's vision of deep ecology—the interconnection between human behavior and the nonhuman environment—as a counter to the neoliberal instrumental denigration of the planet. But it implicated it in an apolitical messianic determinism. Acorn's liberation from Christian America stems not from their collective action, but from events, like global warming, over which they do not have direct control. For example, in *Parable of the Talents* a landslide shuts off power to the command center that controls the slave collars that keep Olamina and her fellow prisoners immobile. And Earthseed's opposition to the inequities of capitalism does not insulate it from becoming trapped within the profit-making enterprise itself. Earthseed becomes incredibly rich in both followers and resources but provincializes its vision for only its truest believers. In a sense, there is a way in which Earthseed's faith in future salvation in space colonization bears an uncanny resemblance to Christian America's proliferation of "dream masks." The masks are virtual-reality headsets that visualize alternative realities (the main character in these is Asha Vere, who fights anti-Christian plots) but become mobilized by state power for thought control.

Still, Butler dramatized the freedom behind Earthseed's ethos of improvisation. Interracial communities exist on the fringes even when they are threatened by white supremacy. So do ephemeral moments of solidarity in spaces unrecognized and unsanctioned in local networks. But improvised secrecy is also what forecloses Acorn from seizing the space of collective transformation precisely as Jarret's power wanes. One of the most vivid ways *Parable* lamented Acorn's failure to expose the link between intersectional oppression and the perpetuation of fundamentalist violence, and its desire to keep it individualized, is through Olamina's decision to settle for an undisclosed monetary sum with Christian America. She takes the money as compensation for her torture under the Crusaders and their crimes of burning women accused of witchcraft as part of what is called the "Pox." Earthseed thus enacted an American brand of pragmatism, which denaturalized truth and foregrounded action as essential for defining social existence. But it still defended an American commitment to self-preservation. Not only because of its strategic concessions to power, but through its focus on gun ownership for self-defense.

Likewise, although Earthseed's vision of Socratic education stood in opposition to the "teachers" at Camp Christian who enforce manual slave labor, its educative goal is anything but open-ended. Acorn seeks to realize positive freedom in citizens through providing basic resources like financed schools, colleges, and scholarships for poor children to achieve a good life serviceable for democratic revitalization. But this is ultimately rooted in an American instrumentalism focused upon rebuilding Acorn through training more doctors and engineers who could build more spaceships. Earthseed's philosophy powerfully denounces American individualism as a violent enterprise. And Acorn embraces a de-Protestantized work ethic based on experimenting with new responses to problems and challenges. As the narrator describes it, "Its promise is not of mansions to live in, milk and honey to drink, or eternal oblivion in some vast whole of nirvana. Its promise is of hard-work and brand-new possibilities, problems, challenges, and changes."[17] But behind this attitude is radical skepticism of government. The fear of being enslaved and recolonized puts Acorn members in a state of heightened panic; they become increasingly worried about everything and everyone they meet.

Olamina's status as a political prophet concerned with questions of the civil sphere, rather than gendered expectations within the private sphere, politicized the role of black women in the utopian tradition. Her status as a "drifter" and refusal to actualize a familial reunion between her and her long-lost daughter, which is a central narrative strain in *Parable of the Talents*, refuse romantic gendered teleology. It is a radical statement about reorganizing the nuclear family. But "hyper-empathy" also makes Olamina into a perfect killer, who is effective at finding her victims and must do so swiftly for fear of feeling their experience of pain. And the melancholic mourning that defines Olamina's thwarted struggle for maternal actualization plays upon gendered myths of difference feminism.

Olamina crystallized *Parable*'s view that the democratic sensibility of Earthseed is both productive and destructive when she asserts that "intelligence is demanding. If it is misdirected by accident or by intent, it can foster its own orgies of breeding and dying."[18] Making questions of rule subject to collective negotiation opposed the tradition of American realism. This position is exemplified by Olamina's brother, Marc. His love of order, security, and stability compels him to join Christian America, even if he doesn't fully share its faith and remains a closeted gay black man. But Earthseed's philosophical antifundamentalism is what leads Olamina to experience what Marc doesn't as she moves from the college lecture circuit, to various stays at friend's homes and in Earthseed communities. This is her sense of homelessness.

In this way, although *Parable* reimagined alienation as emancipatory and community as ephemeral, both only intensify

Olamina's messianic dreams and fundamentalism. At the conclusion of *Parable of the Talents*, she is impervious to social criticism. Earthseed's care ethics countered amoral realism but couldn't escape the very moralism that threatened it. Olamina insists that greater responsibility emerges from a face-to-face ethics, where fellow community members are known and collective accountability emerges beyond the comforts of abstraction. But there is something exclusionary about this communitarianism when shame polices the boundaries of good behavior and the fear of group infiltration and subversion is constant. As Olamina puts it, "Serious misbehavior is harder to get away with, harder even to begin when everyone who sees you knows who you are, where you live, who your family is, and whether you have any business doing what you're doing."[19]

UTOPIA IN RUINS

Parable's dystopian vision has been politically and culturally prophetic. The glimmer of political hope in radical social transformation that many saw in the election of Barack Obama in 2008 was never fulfilled by his pragmatic centrism that was, to some extent, prefigured in the liberalism of Christopher Donner in *Parable of the Sower.* Eight years later, it was all but evaporated with the election of Donald Trump in 2016. Both his campaign rhetoric and policies since have combined the disastrous neoliberal free-marketization, xenophobic militarism, and Christian Right fundamentalism that *Parable of the Talents* prophesized.

More generally, black dystopian culture has deepened *Parable*'s theoretical insights. Among the most notable texts have been Toni Morison's novel *Paradise* (1997), which fictionalized *Parable*'s warning of patriarchy through a black patriarchal community intent on perpetuating its version of black American exceptionalism as violence upon women of color. Jordan Peele's film *Get Out* (2017), a blend of horror and science fiction about white people artificially implanting their brains in and controlling black bodies, continued *Parable*'s meditation on the link between pleasure, fantasy, virtual reality, and domination. A world-renowned public art installation, "The Heidelberg Project," in Detroit, Michigan, curated by Tyree Guyton, has for thirty years chronicled the city's experience. It has done this through juxtaposing found objects like dolls, machinery, and used plastic against clocks to mark the time of black political loss and geographic evisceration. Heidelberg captures Detroit's transformation from a once-exemplary symbol of middle-class decadence into the setting for dystopian fiction. After fifty years of white flight and deindustrialization, Detroit itself looks a lot like *Parable*'s postapocalyptic LA: saturated with burned-down homes, militarized public space, defunded schools, and dysfunctional public infrastructure.

The ending of *Parable* on the note of withdrawal rather than engagement—as its ships' leave to explore human relocation to space—captured Butler's suspicion of utopia. Countercultural philosophical critique was not the same action, utopia could become seduced by power, and the transcendent vision that accounted for its allure was what could cause its failure. In this way *Parable* dramatized in fiction the contradiction black utopia began with one hundred and fifty years before with Martin Delany. Experiments in political escape could never fully abandon ideas that reinforced inequality, but could articulate democratic emancipatory ideas that were never fully realized.

At the same time, by concluding with the image of black space travel—of a form of black liberation through escape from US white supremacy, racism, mass incarceration, poverty, neoliberal capitalism, instrumentalism, and patriarchy—*Parable* ended the twentieth century with the same spirit of hope that had, from the outset, preoccupied black utopians. It found something in the ruins that made dreaming so hard and so urgent: a new beginning in which dignity, flourishing, self-expression, and freedom could become real.

CONCLUSION

Black Utopia and the Contemporary Political Imagination

Over the past several decades, utopian imaginings have largely been abandoned. Contemporary observers may still tolerate the cultural consumption of utopian science fiction and fantasy literature, but they shudder at the thought of realizing political utopia. On some level, this concern has a sound intellectual basis. It is difficult to fully disentangle the dream of communist equality from Stalinist Russia's repressiveness, industrial advancement from the Nazi mechanized slaughter of Jews, unlimited nuclear energy from nuclear war, an end to disease from eugenics. And black antiutopians themselves raised concerns about these dangerous affinities. Freedom can morph into totalitarianism, equality can expunge dissent, perfection can't tolerate imperfection, human triumph masks human finitude. In doing this they dramatized what the philosopher Karl Popper declared: utopia's fruit was nothing but dictatorship, for the idea of realizing an ideal state meant subsuming the good of the whole to the vision of the few. As he put it, "The Utopian attempt to realize an ideal state, using a blueprint of society as a whole, is one which demands a strong centralized rule of a few, and which is therefore likely to lead to a dictatorship."[1] According to this view, if utopia is for dreamers, better it stay that way. For dreams can quickly change into nightmares from which one cannot awaken. Utopia should be abandoned in the dustbin of the violent twentieth century.[2] Summarizing this view as the prevailing orthodoxy of the present, the intellectual historian Russell Jacoby says: "A utopian spirit—a sense that the future could transcend the present—has vanished. . . . The belief is stone dead. . . . There are no alternatives. This is the wisdom of our times, an age of political exhaustion and retreat."[3]

THE SPIRIT OF UTOPIA

But antiutopian skepticism about realizing political utopias shouldn't have a chilling effect on extrapolating a lively political imagination from utopia's languages, landscapes, licenses, losses, inventions, and parables. If utopia were a city, it would be wrong to miss its dwellings for the skyline.[4] In a highly synoptic, even if provocative, account of utopia, the political theorist Judith Shklar made this error, wrongly putting it in a straightjacket, arguing that utopia was nothing but the "moralist's artifact," which assumed a singular truth. As she put it, "utopia . . . is of necessity a changeless harmonious whole, in which a shared recognition of truth unites all citizens. . . . In utopia, there cannot, by definition, be any room for eccentricity."[5] But Shklar's zeal to systematize the hidden truth behind, and organizing intellectual kernel within, utopia made her blind to its eccentric ideas. Her desire to so fully understand utopia on the terms of its truest believers and its most devout citizens precluded her from seeing how utopia could become an important guide for expanding political thought in the here and now.

If utopians are dreamers, then their dreams should be analyzed as such. What Freud taught us through his psychoanalytic model is applicable here: dreams must be understood for the associations their elements conjure in the dreamer.[6] For this perspective, utopia offers practical guidance for the present, especially if we appreciate what the American anarchist Emma Goldman said long ago: "practical" is not something that fits into the world as it is but what eliminates all that is cancerous.[7] Recreating a utopian world in its entirety without any modification is certainly a mistake. But utopian visions and antiutopian critiques can invigorate our democracy—make it more representative of popular interest, more free and egalitarian, less violent and exploitative.[8] To make our world a place in which we would like to live, work, love, and create. A world that has a future with a horizon, not only a past with a long shadow.

This means retaining democratic horizons while abandoning its darkness. It means imagining new utopias but deconstructing their unseen assumptions, unexamined logics, closed corridors, and unknown unknowns. Or, to put it in the words of the philosopher Paul Tillich, "What is important is . . . the idea of utopia that overcomes utopia in its untruth and sustains it in its truth. . . . *It is the spirit of utopia that conquers utopia.*"[9] Reclaiming this spirit means not simply, in the words of Jürgen Habermas, adopting better "norms," which can improve the "facts" that organize contemporary liberal juridical democracies, founded in the rule of law.[10] It means instead expanding and complicating the meaning of and relationship between value and law in ways that test the basic presumptions of political organization.

UTOPIA, CRITIQUE, AND CONTEMPORARY POLITICAL THOUGHT

Energizing contemporary freedom struggles and imagining the impossible require combining the most productive elements of black utopian imagination and antiutopian critique, rather than accepting the false choice between them. It means reclaiming the sense of freedom without dehumanization and accepting the idea of perfectibility without fundamentalism. It means embracing radical equality and resisting gender and sexual domination. And it means taking seriously radical hope in the face of the unknown without messianic deliverance.

Moreover, elite rule must be rejected in favor of popular rule, which needs to be subject to constant scrutiny and revision. Instrumental and technocratic rationality—the automated rule of numbers, statistics, and algorithms—needs to be abandoned in favor of an ethical horizon, which treats citizens as ends deserving of dignity and reclaims the importance of fallibility and experimentation in politics. There is ethical value in a deconstructive ethos that exposes the contradictions and obfuscations of power, but it must exist with a normative horizon from which to make political judgments about justice and liberation. To this end, truthfulness and greater collective understanding cannot be entirely discarded. But truth and knowledge need to both be understood as informed by power.

More specifically, however, black utopian and antiutopian work chastens contemporary American faith in postracialism—that good intentions and better laws could solve the problem of racism, as if it can be remedied through better civic education or harsher penalties for bad deeds. Their work teaches that race thoroughly saturates self-understanding, and that racism requires forgetting the freedom of intimacy and creativity, while enshrining as natural law emotional disconnection and a sense of invulnerability. One cannot see past race because race makes what appears visible. Racism promotes the fantasy that we could avoid the risks of social relationships and the anxiety of worldly impermanence.[11]

From black utopians and antiutopians, we also learn that irreverence toward the boundaries of communities and identities, which can never be fully stabilized, is essential.[12] Loss does productive emancipatory work in a community founded on the capacity for change and flexibility.[13] Arguments about postracialism describe it as either fact (racism no longer governs human life after the victories of the civil rights movement and the election of Barack Obama) or an aspiration rooted in colorblindness (where race is not treated as a salient variable in allocating social resources). Postracialism in black utopia is something else: it is a postracist condition countering the logic of racism—its power binaries, languages, ways of being and organizing collectively. Failure to appreciate the comic dimension of fetishizing and commodifying white and black skin is deadly. From black utopia we also learn that human attachment is much too unwieldy a force and its desires are too disruptive to make the rigid boundaries of race possible. Delinking desire from social scripts makes it more complex in ways that allow for pluralistic expression.

Black utopians and antiutopians further teach that imagining an emancipatory future requires unmooring crisis from its reactionary formulations. Crucial is it to remember that crises usually benefit political elites and entrench existing inequalities by creating a condition in which repression becomes a tactic for assuaging popular fears.[14] But crises ignite opportunities for more revelatory ways of seeing.[15] Interruptions can provide the freedom that they seem to threaten, leading to unexpected changes. Loss gives life, while finitude brings clarity. From this vantage point, pessimistic feelings should be separated from despair about realizing certain goals, but benevolent intentions must be deconstructed in the process.[16] Self-ascribed virtues sometimes have lethal costs. There is a logical dark side of the political realism that some believe only promotes competition over competing desires.[17] Pluralism and democratic conversation are difficult to maintain when one is blind to the way they replicate ideas of the dominant group.

From black utopia we also learn that optimism is not the inevitability of progress but the potential for a more free existence. Freedom must be reconstructed as an opening up of oneself to oneself and, by extension, to the world. Freedom can become a new way of acquiring relationships of fulfillment and agency, of dispensing with fantasies of control and order. Creative discovery of oneself, an opening up of what one didn't know they knew, challenges absolute self-certainty. Only by acting, engaging oneself directly, could one know who they were and what they wanted. This means appreciating the opacity and fleetingness of agency. Freedom is terrifying and beautiful. Its terror can lead to the valorization of arbitrary authority, but its beauty can lead to greater equality.[18]

Black utopian and antiutopian thought further provides lessons for how citizens can cultivate collective power. Violence should be treated with skepticism in achieving political liberation. There is greater value in cultivating an open-ended popular pragmatic politics.[19] Communities become destructive when stabilized, when blood and shared history become barometers for inclusion, when one can no longer recognize its ever-changing forms. Antidemocratic conditions of a perfect society—the degradation of women, the instrumentalist logic of unfettered capitalism, the dismissal of creativity for its own sake—threaten the elevation of those who need it most. Liberation's meaning needs to be recast through the needs of the oppressed, rather than the universalism professed by the powerful. From this perspective, we see why intellectual and political decolonization should become the testing ground for freedom. The lives of the neglected and exploited become the measure for equality.

BLACK UTOPIA NOW

Sustaining the spirit of black utopia is vital for confronting our contemporary global moment. The election of Donald Trump in the United States and the rise of right-wing movements in Europe threaten the vulnerable fabric of democracy in both its liberal and its more socialist iterations. A rise in xenophobia, ethnonationalism, the closing of borders, and the demonization of refugees and Muslims—compounded with a resurgent embrace of economic deregulation, aggressive climate-change denial, and militarization—destroys the possibility for a critical civic society and brings terror to people's everyday lives. This is especially the case for people of color who are most vulnerable in a world still defined by global white supremacy. To make matters worse, the denigration of truth, art, and scientific inquiry and political dissent coexists with a set of Orwellian inversions, which equate national security with mass surveillance and suggest that dissent and freedom require exclusions.

Elements of the mainstream political left seem stunted. Too wedded to a prevailing common sense, they are unable, or unwilling, to confront this. They are debilitated by a nostalgic vision of opposition. They defend free-market privatization, enmesh themselves in dreams of patriotic liberal exceptionalism, and pine for common ground with reactionary forces where none exists. We are repeatedly told that political institutions need gradual reforms and that the free market needs support—perhaps only the occasional helping hand. Or that racial injustice too—police brutality, massive incarceration, and segregation toward black people—will improve over time. But unrevised in this mode of opposition and uncritical hope in progress are the basic assumptions about political imagination.

Our contemporary moment is rife with uncertainty. But if the burgeoning resistance movements against authoritarianism, misogyny, racism, and economic inequality are any indication, popular egalitarian movements will have a powerful voice in what comes in and of the future. Our dystopian postdemocratic political moment requires imaginative thoughts. We need more rather than fewer utopian ideas about radical democracy and social freedom, more rather than fewer antiutopian critiques of American faith in free-market utopianism, religious fundamentalism, technological determinism, and racial progress. Black utopia can add to this chorus trying to generate them.

NOTES

INTRODUCTION

1. For a comprehensive, even if brief, overview of utopianism, see Lyman Tower Sargent, *Utopianism: A Very Short Introduction* (New York: Oxford University Press, 2010). One of Sargent's contributions is dividing utopianism into three categories: literary utopia, utopian practice, and utopian social practice (5).
2. The classic historical survey of utopia is Frank E. Manuel and Fritzie P. Manuel, *Utopian Thought in the Western World* (Cambridge, MA: Belknap Press of Harvard University Press, 1979). As they write, "Before the sixteenth century was out, the adjectival form 'utopian' was born, and when it was not merely a derogatory epithet, connoting a wild fancy or a chimerical notion, it could refer to an ideal psychological condition or to an idealizing capacity. . . . By the early nineteenth century innovative utopian thought had all but lost its enclosed space . . . in these rationalist, systematic utopias whose promise was the whole world, the means of reaching utopia was transformed from an adventure story or a rite of passage to Elysium into a question of political action: How do you change a present misery into a future happiness of this world" (2–3).
3. In his classic text, Melvin Lasky summarizes the utopian political worldview as follows: "The utopians rarely went on to conceive of a free, differentiated man because in an elemental sense they felt men were too devilishly, wastefully, pointlessly free. They hardly hoped for diversity, for differentness among men in society, because their deepest longing was for the miracle of a coherence which could give a measure of purpose, dignity, and meaning to the empty randomness that marked and marred the life they were living." Melvin Lasky, *Utopia and Revolution* (Chicago: University of Chicago Press, 1976), 10.

4. The only explicit survey of utopia in American political thought I am aware of is Harold V. Rhodes, *Utopia in American Political Thought* (Tucson: University of Arizona Press, 1967). Rhodes discusses figures like B. F. Skinner, Upton Sinclair, and Edward Bellamy but pays very little attention to both race and the black American tradition.
5. Hannah Arendt, *The Human Condition* (Chicago: University of Chicago Press, 1958).
6. For a survey of some of the most important utopian American communities, of which the Shakers and Oneida were part, see Chris Jennings, *Paradise Now: The Story of American Utopianism* (New York: Random House, 2016).
7. In his classic study of utopian visions, Fred Polak argues that their overarching concern can be broken down into five basic maxims: "1. Life cannot be purely transitory: there must be something more enduring. Man hopes for future grâce. 2. Life cannot simply end in imperfection. There must be an Other realm into which man can enter. 3. Life should not be transitory and imperfect. Man rebels out of despair, but without hope. 4. Life is not as it appears to be. This world is an illusion and the essential reality is veiled from man. 5. Life does not have to be the way it is. Man can reform and re-create the world after any image he chooses." Fred Polak, *The Image of the Future* (New York: Elsevier, 1973), 2.
8. Ernst Bloch, *The Spirit of Utopia* (Palo Alto: Stanford University Press, 2000), 3.
9. In the words of George Kateb, we should understand the utopian imagination as one that asks, what if there existed "harmony within the soul of each man, harmony of each man with all others?" George Kateb, *Utopia and Its Enemies* (New York: Free Press of Glencoe, 1963), 9.
10. Frye, "Varieties of Literary Utopias," in *Utopias and Utopian Thought*, ed. Frank E. Manuel (Boston: Beacon, 1967), 25.
11. Black American utopian thought is notably missing from studies of utopia. Sargent's *Utopianism* doesn't mention any African American thinkers in detail, while a new text on utopian thought for democratic life—S. D. Chrostowska and James D. Ingram, eds., *Political Uses of Utopia: New Marxist, Anarchist, and Radical Democratic Perspectives* (New York: Columbia University Press, 2016)—has no discussion of race or black utopian thought. The exploration that comes the closest to this is Robin D. G. Kelley, *Freedom Dreams: The Black Radical Imagination* (Boston: Beacon, 2003), which focuses on the history of the black diaspora's reflections on communism, surrealism, radical feminism, and reparations. This book shares with Kelley's a concern to decipher some

visions that could be labeled utopian for energizing contemporary political life. At the same time, my focus is on many figures unexplored by Kelley and more seriously examines the notion of utopian literary and social theories in African American thought and culture, while placing them into conversation with questions that concern political theorists. An important book, which seems to gesture toward a black utopian study, Wilson J. Moses, *Afrotopia: The Roots of African American Popular History* (New York: Cambridge University Press, 1998), is largely a study of Afrocentric narratives of the African past, which are, according to Moses, a form of "utopia" because they see "Africans" as the "most advanced people on earth" (42). Other books that examine aspects of black radicalism—ranging from black Marxism to black nationalism—fail to place these movements into conversation with the ideas that emerge in black utopian literature, art, or poetry, including Michael C. Dawson, *Black Visions: The Roots of Contemporary African-American Political Ideologies* (Chicago: University of Chicago Press, 2001); Anthony Bogues, *Black Heretics, Black Prophets: Radical Political Intellectuals* (New York: Routledge, 2003); Cedric J. Robinson, *Black Marxism: The Making of the Black Radical Tradition* (Chapel Hill: University of North Carolina Press, 2000); Wilson J. Moses, *The Golden Age of Black Nationalism, 1850–1925* (New York: Oxford University Press, 1988); Sterling Stuckey, *The Ideological Origins of Black Nationalism* (Boston: Beacon, 1972).

12. Some of this is detailed well in Eddie Glaude, *Exodus! Religion, Race and Nation in Early Nineteenth-Century Black America* (Chicago: University of Chicago Press, 2000).
13. For this, see William H. Pease and Jane Pease, *Black Utopia: Negro Communal Experiments in America* (Madison: State Historical Society of Wisconsin, 1963).
14. See Mark Dery, "Black to the Future," in *Flame Wars: The Discourse of Cyberculture*, ed. Mark Dery (Durham: Duke University Press, 1994), 182–85.
15. See Richard Iton, *In Search of the Black Fantastic: Politics and Popular Culture in the Post-Civil Rights Era* (New York: Oxford University Press, 2011).
16. Paul Gilroy, *The Black Atlantic: Modernity and Double Consciousness* (Cambridge, MA: Harvard University Press, 1995).
17. Not surprisingly, then, racial inequality was often ignored and slavery was smuggled in—think, for instance, of Aristotle insisting in the *Politics*, which outlined his ideal middle-class *politiea* of constitutional rule, that it was both natural and beneficial, while in More's *Utopia*, slavery,

though considered a more humane punishment than death, is justified. For a historical overview, see George Frederickson, *Racism: A Short History* (Princeton: Princeton University Press, 2009). For a rich theoretical account, see Utz McKnight, *Race and the Politics of Exception: Equality, Sovereignty and American Democracy* (New York: Routledge, 2013).

18. Lewis Gordon, *An Introduction to Africana Philosophy* (New York: Cambridge University Press, 2008), 76.
19. G. W. F. Hegel, *Lectures on the Philosophy of World History*, trans. H. B. Nisbet (Cambridge: Cambridge University Press, 1975), 176.
20. See Max Weber, *The Protestant Ethic and the Spirit of Capitalism* (New York: Routledge, 2001).
21. Wilson J. Moses, *Creative Conflict in African American Thought* (Cambridge: Cambridge University Press, 2004).
22. Another reason why communism is not treated with much depth in this study is because there has been excellent work done on this tradition by historians like Kelley in *Freedom Dreams*, by sociologists like Robinson in *Black Marxism*, as well as by philosophers who consider the links between class and race, like Charles Mills in *From Class to Race: Essays in White Marxism and Black Radicalism* (Lanham, MD: Rowman and Littlefield, 2003). At the same time, I would argue that, unlike the figures discussed here, much of the vision of utopia within black communism in figures like Hubert Harrison, Cyril Briggs, Hosea Hudson, and Richard B. Moore is, as with Marx, left open-ended and not specified. For an excellent account of black literary figures who either identified as or were deemed communists in the 1950s, see Mary Helen Washington, *The Other Blacklist: The African American Literary and Cultural Left of the 1950s* (New York: Columbia University Press, 2013).
23. See James C. Scott, *Domination and the Arts of Resistance: Hidden Transcripts* (New Haven: Yale University Press, 1993).
24. For a sociological study of this idea through a specific focus on the memory of slavery, see Ron Eyerman, *Cultural Trauma: Slavery and the Formation of African American Identity* (Cambridge: Cambridge University Press, 2002).
25. See Susan Buck-Morss, *Dreamworld and Catastrophe: The Passing of Mass Utopia in East and West* (Cambridge, MA: MIT Press, 2002).
26. See Theodor Adorno, *Minima Moralia: Reflections on a Damaged Life* (New York: Verso, 2006).
27. My method in this book tries to blend elements of various methodologies. I am sympathetic to Sheldon Wolin's approach in his classic *Politics and Vision*, which tries to situate historic political ideas in their

context—as opposed to simply historicizing them without any sense of the contemporary moment. See Sheldon Wolin, *Politics and Vision: Continuity and Innovation in Western Political Thought* (Princeton: Princeton University Press, 2016). At the same time, however, I try to draw insight from the important strain of Afro-Caribbean and African philosophy, which tries to creolize the very idea of the canon. "Creolization" involves reading various Western and non-Western texts (usually Euro-modern or Afro-Modern) alongside one another, with the goal of demonstrating not incommensurable differences, but unexpected affinities that can be theoretically generative. For some important accounts of this in action, see Paget Henry, *Caliban's Reason: Introducing Afro-Caribbean Philosophy* (New York: Routledge, 2000); Gordon, *An Introduction to Africana Philosophy*; Jane Gordon, *Creolizing Political Theory: Reading Rousseau Through Fanon* (New York: Fordham University Press, 2014).

28. See Karl Mannheim, *Ideology and Utopia: Introduction to the Sociology of Knowledge* (New York: Harvest, 1965).
29. This book makes a contribution to the literature on the way that African American political thought expands political theory and American thought. Nick Bromell, *The Time Is Always Now: Black Thought and the Transformation of US Democracy* (New York: Oxford University Press, 2013); Jack Turner, *Awakening to Race: Individualism and Social Consciousness in America* (Chicago: University of Chicago Press, 2012); Danielle S. Allen, *Talking to Strangers: Anxieties of Citizenship After Brown v. Board of Education* (Chicago: University of Chicago Press, 2004); Alex Zamalin, *African American Political Thought and American Culture: The Nation's Struggle for Racial Justice* (New York: Palgrave Macmillan, 2015); Zamalin, *Struggle on Their Minds: The Political Thought of African American Resistance* (New York: Columbia University Press, 2017); Christopher Lebron, *The Making of Black Lives Matter: A Brief History of an Idea* (New York: Oxford University Press, 2017).

1. MARTIN DELANY'S EXPERIMENT IN ESCAPE

1. Paul Gilroy famously argued that "Delany is a figure of extraordinary complexity whose political trajectory through abolitionisms and emigrationisms, from Republicans to Democrats, dissolves any simple attempt to fix him as consistently either conservative or radical." See Paul Gilroy, *The Black Atlantic: Modernity and Double Consciousness* (Cambridge, MA: Harvard University Press, 1995), 20. For a recent comprehensive

overview of Delany's thought throughout his life, see Tunde Adekele, *Without Regard to Race: The Other Martin Robison Delany* (Jackson: University Press of Mississippi, 2009).

2. Martin Delany, *The Condition, Elevation, Emigration and Destiny of the Colored People of the United States* (Baltimore: Black Classic, 1991), 183.
3. Along the most famous first biographies of this time were Victor Ullman, *Martin Delany: The Beginnings of Black Nationalism* (Boston: Beacon, 1971) and Dorothy Sterling, *The Making of an Afro-American: Martin Robison Delany, 1812–1885* (Garden City, NY: Da Capo, 1971). Delany's thought has been most extensively examined by literary critics, historians, sociologists, and cultural critics. The only comprehensive political-philosophical account of Delany's thought—and still the most important—is Tommie Shelby's essay "Two Conceptions of Black Nationalism." Shelby's concern is to reconstruct Delany's political thought to expose the tension between his own classical black nationalism, which sees the destiny of black people to be redeemed through a shared homeland and fate, and pragmatic black nationalism, which sees it as a response to white supremacy. Shelby is interested in delineating Delany's explicit views and arguments to shed light on the avenues for black politics, but I want to explore what Delany's meditations on utopian political possibility reveal about his understanding of ideal citizenship. See Tommie Shelby, "Two Conceptions of Black Nationalism: Martin Delany on the Meaning of Black Solidarity," *Political Theory* 31, no. 5 (2003): 664–92.
4. Almost all readings of *Blake* have been by literary critics, who try to situate its relevance in the history of black and American literature. Eric J. Sundquist reads it, alongside Herman Melville's *Benito Cereno*, as a narrative of black self-making and resistance in *To Wake the Nations: Race in the Making of American Literature* (Cambridge, MA: Harvard University Press, 1993), chap. 2. And Robert S. Levine argues that "Delany's vision of the crucial role that could be played by an intelligent, full-blooded leader (like himself) in creating a Pan-African community in the Americans (and beyond) is the central subject [of the novel]." Robert Levine, *Martin Delany, Frederick Douglass, and the Politics of Representative Identity* (Chapel Hill: University of North Carolina Press, 1997). In this chapter, however, I try to show how the novel reveals a political theory.
5. Nell Irvin Painter is therefore right that Delany was intoxicated by the ideas of the American ruling elite. As she puts it, he embraced "American ideals like leadership by elites . . . [or] his faith in private enterprise

that also appears in the thought of Booker T. Washington. . . . The secret of Delany's leadership lay in in his eloquent espousal of purely American ideals purged of racism and racial subjugation. Delany spoke for men and women who considered themselves the best of the race, fitted through relative wealth and education to lead the black masses." See Nell Irvin Painter, "Martin Delany: Elitism and Black Nationalism," in *Black Leaders of the Nineteenth Century*, ed. Leon Litwack and August Meier (Urbana: University of Illinois Press, 1991), 150.

6. Delany's call for black emigration had a divine theological tinge of manifest destiny, "God has, as certain as he has ever designed any thing, designed this great portion of the New World, for us, the colored races; and as certain as we stubborn our hearts, and stiffen our necks against it, his protecting arm and fostering care will be withdrawn from us." Delany, *The Condition*, 183.
7. Martin Delany, *Blake; or the Huts of America* (Cambridge, MA: Harvard University Press, 2017), 22.
8. It should perhaps be noted that I would distinguish what we might call Delany's realism or conservatism from what Tommie Shelby describes as his pragmatism. The pragmatist flexibly changes their means depending on the ends they want to reach; the conservative realist is someone who internalizes the reality of a given social structure and tries to construct a politics using that social structure's terms. Shelby's definition of black pragmatism, or what he calls black solidarity, is something that urges "black solidarity and concerted action as a political strategy to lift or resist oppression. This could of course mean forming a self-governing black nation-state or a separate self determining community within a multinational state, but it could also mean working to create a racially integrated society or even a 'postracial' polity (i.e., a political order where 'race' has no social meaning). . . . Solidaristic commitment of pragmatic nationalism is based on a desire to live in a just society, a society that need not be, or even contain, a self-determining black community." See Shelby, Two Conceptions of Black Nationalism," 667.
9. Delany, *The Condition*, 42.
10. In this way, he echoed the argument of American individualist par excellence Benjamin Franklin, who thought instrumental activity could bring happiness, where one disciplined their body and mind to achieve greater wealth and honor. See Benjamin Franklin, "Way to Wealth," in *Autobiography, and Other Writings*, ed. Ormond Seavey (Oxford: Oxford University Press, 2008), 267.

11. Delany, *The Condition*, 42.
12. Karl Marx and Friedrich Engels, "The Manifesto of the Communist Party," in *The Marx-Engels Reader*, ed. Robert C. Tucker (New York: Norton, 1978), 469–500.
13. Delany, *The Condition*, 192–93.
14. Delany, 155.
15. Delany, 11.
16. Delany, 19.
17. For Jefferson, see Thomas Jefferson, *Notes on the State of Virginia* (Boston: Lily and Wait, 1832), especially "Query XIV," 135–56.
18. Delany, *The Condition*, 155–56.
19. Ralph Waldo Emerson, *Political Writings* (Cambridge: Cambridge University Press, 2008), 165.
20. Delany, *Blake*, 66.
21. Delany, 88.
22. Delany, *The Condition*, 42.
23. Delany, *Blake*, 15.
24. Delany, *The Condition*, 48–49.
25. Delany, 42–43.
26. Examples of this could be found throughout *Blake*. See, for example, pages 128, 129, 167–68, 189. On the one hand, Robert Levine is right to the extent that Delany's thought wasn't completely governed by rigid notions of black masculinity. He writes that "Delany operated within the conventional gender discourses of the time in which fully enfranchised citizenship was defined in relation to manhood"; it is noteworthy that "he challenged patriarchical ideology. He regularly wrote of the importance of education to Women, urging women to take their places as political and economic leaders." On the other hand, his work shows that masculinity, individualism, and instrumentalism are deeply connected and can't easily be severed. See Levine, *Martin Delany*, 19.
27. Delany, *Blake*, 264.
28. G. W. F. Hegel, *The Phenomenology of Spirit*, trans. A. V. Miller (New York: Oxford University Press, 1977), 111–18.
29. Hegel, 64–65.
30. Delany, *Blake*, 305.
31. Delany, 45.
32. Delany, 199.
33. Delany, 28–31.
34. Delany, 259.
35. Delany, *The Condition*, 50.

36. Delany, *Blake*, 101.
37. Delany, 312.
38. Delany, 103.
39. Delany, 20.
40. Martin Delany, *Principa of Ethnology: The Origin of Races and Color* (Philadelphia: Harper, 1880), 105.
41. Delany, *The Condition*, 187.
42. www.gutenberg.org/files/22118/22118-h/22118-h.htm, 108.
43. http://docsouth.unc.edu/church/cooper/cooper.html, 31.

2. TURN-OF-THE-CENTURY BLACK LITERARY UTOPIANISM

1. For an important literary text that surveys these four texts from the perspective of utopian racial passing, see Giula Fabi, *Passing and the Rise of the African American Novel* (Urbana: University of Illinois Press, 2001), chap. 2. Unlike Fabi, I am interested in the political ideas of these texts more so than their attempts to reimagine black identity.
2. As the literary critics Tess Chakkalal and Kenneth Warren note, "Griggs was remarkably consistent in his political opinions. Against the rising tide of antiblack sentiment during the period, Griggs believed that cooperation between the races remained the best and most effective policy. To secure such cooperation, however, he was often willing to speak up even when other prominent black spokespersons held their tongues." In Tess Chakkalal and Kenneth Warren, eds., *Jim Crow, Literature, and the Legacy of Sutton E. Griggs* (Athens: University of Georgia Press, 2013), 7.
3. The best and most comprehensive overview of Harper's work remains Melba J. Boyd, *Discarded Legacy: Politics and Poetics in the Life of Frances E. W. Harper, 1825–1911* (Detroit: Wayne State University Press, 1994).
4. For a critical introduction of Hopkins, see Hazel V. Carby, "Introduction," in *The Magazine Novels of Pauline Hopkins*, ed. Henry Louis Gates, Jr. (Oxford: Oxford University Press, 1988), xxix–l; and Hanna Wallinger, *Pauline Hopkins: A Literary Biography* (Athens: University of Georgia Press, 2012).
5. Despite the African American public intellectual Cornel West's short introduction to a recent version of *Imperium*, Griggs's work has been overlooked as a source not only of utopian thought, but of a rich political theory that should be firmly placed in the American canon. Most of the work on Griggs has been done by literary critics and intellectual

historians. This chapter aims to help address what Chakkalal and Warren say about Griggs's work: "We still have much to learn about who Griggs was and how his books helped to shape African American literary culture at the turn of the twentieth century." Chakkalal and Warren, *Jim Crow, Literature, and the Legacy of Sutton E. Griggs*, 8.

6. For the defense of the American Revolution as purely political, as opposed to socioeconomic, see Hannah Arendt, *On Revolution* (New York: Penguin, 2006).
7. For a historical view of the development of this sphere, see Jürgen Habermas, *The Structural Transformation of the Public Sphere: An Inquiry Into a Category of Bourgeois Society* (Cambridge, MA: MIT Press, 1991).
8. Frances Harper, *Iola Leroy; or, Shadows Uplifted* (New York: Dover, 2010), 251.
9. Sutton E. Griggs, *Imperium in Imperio* (New York: Modern Library, 2004), 145.
10. For a history of this moment, see Michael Kazin, *The Populist Persuasion: An American History* (Ithaca: Cornell University Press, 1998).
11. For one of the classic works on the development of black feminist fiction, see Hazel Carby, *Reconstructing Womanhood: The Emergence of the Afro-American Woman Novelist* (New York: Oxford University Press, 1989).
12. Griggs, *Imperium*, 93. The novel's depiction of this as nothing but black emasculation exposes the novel's queerphobic underpinnings, while missing the particular intersectional reality of black women's exploitation—both of which, with very few exceptions, were regretfully common in late-nineteenth-century American thought. But Griggs's indictment of white America couldn't have been clearer: blackness is treated as an object to be manipulated and exploited at will.
13. See Gene Andrew Jarrett, *Representing the Race: A New Political History of African American Literature* (New York: New York University Press, 2011), 73–101.
14. The literary critic Susan Gilman is right that Dixon and Griggs can partly be read as writers, in radically different ways and for different ends, that employed in the 1890s what she calls "the melodramatic," which provides a "historiographic mode that reframes U.S. history in racial terms. . . . They focus as much on politics, class, and economics as on race and nation and as much on intraracial divisions and collectivities as on interracial conflict" (75). Nonetheless, while she positions Griggs's work as a "New Negro" response to Dixon's white supremacy when she says, "in explicit contrast to the 'fawning, sniffling, cowardly Negro,' of slavery,

Griggs's 'New Negro' confronts white violence as a recurrence of the intimidation and lynching of the Reconstruction Klan" (84), she doesn't fully consider how Griggs's own work complexly rehashes apolitical racist images in an effort to make claims about, and for the sake of, liberation. See Susan Gilman, *Blood Talk: American Race Melodrama and the Culture of the Occult* (Chicago: University of Chicago Press, 2003).

15. Griggs, *Imperium*, 154.
16. Griggs, 36.
17. Griggs, 143.
18. Griggs, 143.
19. Griggs, 145.
20. Griggs, 141.
21. Edward A. Johnson, *Light Ahead for the Negro* (New York: Grafton, 1904), 80.
22. See Wiebe, *The Search for Order, 1877–1920* (New York: Hill and Wang, 1967).
23. Griggs, *Imperium*, 141.
24. Johnson, *Light Ahead for the Negro*, 76.
25. Griggs, *Imperium*, 119.
26. Pauline Hopkins, *Of One Blood; or the Hidden Self* (New York: Washington Square, 2004), 178.
27. Griggs, *Imperium*, 164.
28. Griggs, 164.

3. W. E. B. DU BOIS'S WORLD OF UTOPIAN INTIMACY

1. Among the best overviews of Du Bois's life is David Levering-Lewis, *W. E. B. Du Bois: A Biography, 1868–1863* (New York: Holt, 2009).
2. As Dora Ahmad argues, "Taken as a whole, Du Bois's oeuvre offers an extended meditation on the nature of hope." See Dora Ahmad, *Landscapes of Hope: Anti-Colonial Utopianism in America* (New York: Oxford University Press, 2009), 146.
3. "The Comet," has not received sustained treatment from political theorists, perhaps because it is seen to be a fictional piece distinct from Du Bois's political-theoretical assumptions, while *Dark Princess* has begun to receive more attention, especially in Juliet Hooker's recent book *Theorizing Race in the Americas*. As she has argued, Du Bois's fictions (she focuses on *Dark Princess* to argue that it is a "form of speculative mestizo

futurism that nevertheless did not romanticize mixture as a solution to racism" [116]) represent the height of his futuristic, utopian thinking. See Juliet Hooker, *Theorizing Race in the Americas: Douglass, Sarmiento, Du Bois, and Vasconcelos* (New York: Oxford University Press, 2017).

4. Du Bois, "The Comet," in *Darkwater: Voices from Within the Veil* (New York: Dover, 2009), 152–53.
5. He developed this idea in one of his earliest and most controversial essays, Du Bois, "The Conservation of Races" (1897).
6. Du Bois.
7. Reiland Rabaka offers a persuasive reading of "The Comet," in dialogue with critical race theory, by arguing that the story is an account of the persistence of white supremacy, even within utopia. As he writes, "Even in utopia blacks can never forget the lived-experiences and life-lessons of the former anti-black world." Rieland Rabaka, "WEB Dubois's 'The Comet' and contributions to Critical Race Theory: An Essay on Black Radical Politics and Anti-Racist Social Ethics," *Ethnic Studies Review* 29, no. 1:36.
8. As much as the story was an account of what Ronald Sundstrum calls an ironic stance toward race—showing its pathology and absurdity and the distortion of the American racist culture—it also framed the productive potential for white racism becoming renounced. See Ronald R. Sundstrom, "The Prophetic and Pragmatic Philosophy of 'Race' in WEB Du Bois's 'The Comet,'" *APA Newsletter on Philosophy and the Black Experience* 99, no. 1 (Fall 1999).
9. Du Bois, "The Comet," 157.
10. Du Bois, 152–53.
11. As he put it, "they flew toward the cable office on the east side, leaving the world of wealth and prosperity for the world of poverty and work." Du Bois, 156.
12. As Levinas put it, "The being that expresses itself imposes itself . . . [and] does so precisely by appealing to me with its destitution and nudity—its hunger—without my being able to be deaf to that appeal." See Emanuel Levinas, *Totality and Infinity: An Essay on Exteriority* (Pittsburgh: Duquesne Press, 1969), 200.
13. Du Bois, "The Comet," 157.
14. Du Bois, 155.
15. His essay in *Darkwater* "The Souls of White Folk" gave theoretical texture to Julia's fears when he wrote, "they preach and strut and shout and threaten, crouching as they clutch at rags of facts and fancies to hide their nakedness" See Du Bois, *Darkwater*, 17.

16. See the critique of this in Hazel Carby, *Race Men* (Cambridge, MA: Harvard University Press, 2000), 9–45.
17. As he put it in his essay "The Damnation of Women," a woman "must have a life work and economic independence. She must have knowledge. She must have the right of motherhood at her own discretion. The present mincing horror at free womanhood must pass if we are ever to be rid of the bestiality of free manhood; not by guarding the weak in weakness do we gain strength, but by making weakness free and strong." Du Bois, *Darkwater*, 96.
18. Du Bois, "The Comet," 158.
19. For Du Bois's relationship to Garvey, see Levering-Lewis, *W. E. B. Du Bois*, 416–34.
20. See Levering-Lewis, 491.
21. W. E. B. Du Bois, *Dark Princess* (Jackson: University Press of Mississippi, 1995), 31.
22. Du Bois, 61.
23. Du Bois, 102.
24. See Ahmad, *Landscapes of Hope*, 156; Du Bois, *Dark Princess*, 112. Interpreters of *Dark Princess* have been split on the novel's gender politics. While some insist that the novel essentializes black femininity and constructs a feminized, Orientalized image of Afro-Asiastic culture; others, like Hooker, have claimed that Du Bois's construction of women as both sexless and self-interested—while problematic—nonetheless also challenges the politics of black respectability that were crucial during the time. For these debates, see Hooker, *Theorizing Race in the Americas*, 139.
25. Du Bois, *Dark Princess*, 126.
26. Kenneth W. Warren is right that the text functions to justify Du Bois's account of talented-tenth politics—and does an astute job connecting it to Du Bois's political thought—but nonetheless, I think, he offers a reading that misses its complex depiction of popular agency. As he writes, "But as one can see in the messianism that dominates his work, from *Darkwater* to *Dark Princess*, and is present in his thinking as early as *The Souls of Black Folk*, maintaining a democratic vision that did not realize its highest expression in the figure of the heroic leader was an ongoing struggle within Du Bois's political thought" (158). See Kenneth W. Warren, "An Inevitable Drift?: Oligarchy, Du Bois, and the Politics of Race Between the Wars," *Boundary 2* 27, no. 3 (2000): 153–69. For a more comprehensive argument about Du Bois's lifelong elitism, see Adolph Reed, *W. E. B. Du Bois and American Political Thought: Fabianism and the Color Line* (New York: Oxford University Press, 1999).

27. As Kautilya put its, "I believe in democracy . . . [but] we common people are so stupid, so forgetful, so selfish." Du Bois, *Dark Princess*, 283.
28. Du Bois, 222, 223.
29. Du Bois, 224.
30. Du Bois, 225.
31. Du Bois, 227.
32. Du Bois, *Darkwater*, 162.
33. Du Bois, 82.
34. For the best account of Du Bois's democratic theory, which my reading of *Dark Princess* borrows from in trying to see which of Du Bois's ideas can be made valuable for democracy rather than whether Du Bois was a democrat, see Lawrie Balfour, *Democracy's Reconstruction: Thinking Politically with W. E. B. Du Bois* (New York: Oxford University Press, 2011).
35. Balfour, 2.

4. GEORGE S. SCHUYLER, IRONY, AND UTOPIA

1. Political theorists—like literary critics—have strikingly ignored Schuyler's political thought precisely because of his archconservatism. This omission may have to do with the very reason literary critics were so reticent to take him seriously. As the literary critic and theorist Jeffrey Ferguson writes, in *The Sage of Sugar Hill*, in what still remains the seminal assessment of Schuyler's life and work, "Considering the evidence for Schuyler's importance as an intellectual figure, we might wonder why his story has not received more detailed academic attention. The answer to this question may well be reduced to a single incident when Schuyler said the wrong thing, in the wrong tone, about the wrong man, at the wrong time: 'Dr. King's principal contribution to world peace has been to roam the country like some sable Typhoid Mary infecting the mentally disturbed with perversion of Christian doctrine and grabbing fat lecture fees from the shallow-pated.'" Schuyler wrote this one month before Martin Luther King, Jr., accepted the 1964 Nobel Peace Prize." See Jeffrey B. Ferguson, *The Sage of Sugar Hill: George S. Schuyler and the Harlem Renaissance* (New Haven: Yale University Press, 2008), 2.
2. The African American novelist Ishmael Reed has called *Black No More* "what might be the most scathing fiction about race written by an American." We could add to this assessment that it may have been the

most searing indictment of American culture. See Ishmael Reed, "Introduction," in *Black No More: Being an Account of Strange and Wonderful Workings of Science in the Land of the Free, A.D. 1933–1940*, by George S. Schuyler (New York: Modern Library, 1999), x.

3. For an account of this sociological school and its view on race, see Dean E. Robinson, *Black Nationalism in American Politics and Thought* (Cambridge: Cambridge University Press, 2001), 105–9.
4. Schuyler, *Black No More*, 4.
5. Schuyler, 9.
6. For this history, see Michael J. Pfeifer, *Rough Justice: Lynching and American Society, 1874–1947* (Urbana: University of Illinois Press, 2004).
7. Friedrich Nietzsche, *The Gay Science* (New York: Vintage, 2010), 273.
8. Schuyler, *Black No More*, 176.
9. Schuyler, 165.
10. Schuyler, 179.
11. Schuyler, 29.
12. Schuyler, 19.
13. Schuyler, 19.
14. Schuyler, 51.
15. For a history of the renaissance, see Nathan Irvin Higgins, *The Harlem Renaissance* (New York: Oxford University Press, 1972).
16. Schuyler, *Black No More*, 26.
17. Schuyler, 75.
18. Schuyler, 130–31.
19. Schuyler, 95.
20. Schuyler, 99.
21. Schuyler, 141–42.
22. Schuyler, 155.
23. For a detailed exploration of this, see Sonnet Retman, "Black No More: George Schuyler and Racial Capitalism," *PMLA* 123, no. 5 (October 2008): 1448–64. As she argues, the novel shows how "race is manufactured and regulated through several kinds of reproduction in the novel, including assembly-line mass production, theatrical staging, and biological procreation. The scientific invention of Black No-More harnesses performance and mechanically reproductive technologies to the making of race, thereby usurping the racialized function of maternal labor. . . . *Black No More* illuminates new market possibilities for the trade of racial property in commodity form during the Fordist era. In this way, Schuyler's narrative offers a complex and prescient understanding of race and

capitalism in the interwar period, one that portends our contemporary negotiations with mass-mediated identity and consumer culture on a global scale" (1449).

24. Schuyler, *Black No More*, 180.
25. As Hill and Rasmussen point out, "The *Black Empire* stories may indeed have been a cynical joke that Schuyler played on his reader, or a whimsical fantasy written for his private amusement." At the same time, they argue that "*Black Empire* reveals Schuyler as a complex and radical thinker, whose ideological journey toward conservatism was more labyrinthine and problematical than has been appreciated." See Robert A. Hill and Kent Rasmussen, "Afterward," in *Black Empire*, by George S. Schuyler (Boston: Northeastern University Press, 1993), 260, 262.
26. This is captured through the words of Patricia Givens, a pilot for the Internationale, who tells its secretary, Carl Slater, that its leader, Dr. Blesidus, realizes black people are intellectually equal to whites. See Schuyler, *Black Empire*, 246. We could read Schuyler's work, in conjunction with *Black Empire* as doing what Alexander M. Bain argues: "that his columns and serials strove to reorient debates about global collectivity from the field of culture to the field of economic interests and citizenship." Alexander M. Bain, "Shocks Americana: George Schuyler Serializes Black Internationalism," *American Literary History* 19, no. 4 (Winter 2007): 937–63, at 941.
27. Schuyler, *Black Empire*, 10.
28. Schuyler, 47.
29. Schuyler, 11.
30. Schuyler, 14.
31. Schuyler, 68.
32. *Black Empire* thus anticipated Theodor Adorno and Max Horkheimer's *Dialectic of Enlightenment* (1944), which connected Enlightenment thinking to totalitarianism. Theodor Adorno and Max Horkheimer, *Dialectic of Enlightenment* (Palo Alto: Stanford University Press, 2007).
33. Schuyler, *Black Empire*, 68.
34. Schuyler, 15.
35. Schuyler, 142.
36. Schuyler, 65.
37. Schuyler, 151.
38. Schuyler, 94.
39. Schuyler, 130.
40. Schuyler, 235.

5. WRIGHT'S *BLACK POWER* AND ANTICOLONIAL ANTIUTOPIANISM

1. See Kevin Gaines, *African Americans in Ghana: Black Expatriates and the Civil Rights Era* (Chapel Hall: University of North Carolina Press, 2008).
2. Richard Wright, *Black Power* (New York: Vintage, 2008), 85–86.
3. For a detailed account of Wright's travels—some of which was omitted in *Black Power*—see what remains one of the finest treatments of Wright's life, Hazel Rowley, *Richard Wright: The Life and Times* (Chicago: University of Chicago Press, 2008), 416–38.
4. For an overview of these two positions, see Kevin Gaines, "Revisiting Richard Wright in Ghana: Black Radicalism and the Dialectics of Diaspora," *Social Text* 67, vol. 19, no. 2 (Summer 2001): 75–101. Gaines himself argues that "despite the considerable problems of Black Power, Wright demands our attention for his revisionist reading of the condition of blacks in the diaspora, which he understands dialectically as the product of slavery, dispersion, and oppression, and simultaneously, as the necessary condition for black modernity and the forging of an anti-imperialist critique of Western culture" (75).
5. For this school of "racial liberalism," see Walter A. Jackson, *Gunnar Myrdal and America's Conscience: Social Engineering and American Liberalism, 1938–1987* (Chapel Hill: University of North Carolina Press, 1990).
6. His anthropological reflections on traditional African culture in *Black Power* revised both Freud's thinking and psychoanalysis in black literature. Most interpretations of *Black Power* try to contextualize it within Wright's oeuvre or situate it within the historical context of the burgeoning African anticolonial movements of the 1950s. However, this chapter joins interpretations of *Black Power* that try to consider its political theoretical value. For a reading that rightly emphasizes how *Black Power* fuses psychoanalysis and colonial critique, see Dorothy Stringer, "Psychology and Black Liberation in Richard Wright's *Black Power*." In that text, she claims, "Paying close attention to the effects of colonial economic control on daily life, Wright discusses such classically psychoanalytic concepts as the return of the repressed, the Oedipal conflict, and anal eroticism in terms of West African daily life, often considerably revising both Freudian concepts and his own notion of black identity in the process" (106). See Dorothy Stringer, "Psychology and Black Liberation in Richard Wright's Black Power," *Journal of Modern Literature* 32, no. 4 (Summer 2009): 105–24.

7. Freud militated against the utopian wish of a world in which pleasure could reign supreme, but his concern with mining the contradictory recesses of the self was nothing short of a continuation of the Enlightenment utopian project of greater self-knowledge. This tension is unpacked in Frank E. Manuel and Fritzie P. Manuel, *Utopian Thought in the Western World* (Cambridge, MA: Belknap Press of Harvard University Press, 1979), 788–92.
8. Wright, *Black Power*, 38, 36.
9. Mary Louise Pratt in *Imperial Eyes* argues that one of the goals of *Black Power* was "trying to represent an experience of ignorance, disorientation, incomprehension, self-dissolution which does not give rise to terror of madness, but rather to a serene receptivity and intense eroticism." Mary Louise Pratt, *Imperial Eyes: Travel Writing and Transculturation* (New York: Routledge, 2007), 218.
10. Wright, *Black Power*, 18.
11. Rowley, *Richard Wright*, 335–45.
12. For a short overview of the "negritude" movement, see Richard Bell, *Understanding African Philosophy* (New York: Routledge, 2002), 21–37.
13. See Michel Fabre, *The World of Richard Wright* (Jackson: University of Mississippi Press, 1985), 192–215.
14. Wright, *Black Power*, 150; Frantz Fanon, *The Wretched of the Earth* (New York: Grove, 2005).
15. Wright, *Black Power*, 157.
16. Wright, 19.
17. Wright, 33–34.
18. Wright, 184.
19. See Rowley, *Richard Wright*, 116–18, 315–17.
20. He said, "I'd have to learn to accept without thought a whole new range of assumptions. Intellectually, I understood my friend's all too clear explanation of why boys liked to hold hands and dance together, yet the sight of it provoked in me a sense of uneasiness on levels of emotion deeper than I could control." Wright, *Black Power*, 141.
21. As he put it, "these lost and sinful girls . . . were the only free people in the entire islands. . . . Without doubt they were the only real democrats within reach. They were genial and they accepted everybody regardless of race, creed, or color; that is, for a price." Wright, *Black Power*, 42. As Stringer correctly argues, "Unnamed women recur again and again across *Black Power* . . . selling oranges, dancing, watching children, doing secretarial work, asking to be taken to the movies, drinking rum, nursing

babies." Stringer, "Psychology and Black Liberation in Richard Wright's *Black Power*," 115.

22. Wright, *Black Power*, 76.
23. Malcolm X, "OAAU Founding Rally," in *By Any Means Necessary* (New York: Pathfinder, 1992), 63.
24. Wright, *Black Power*, 78.
25. Senghor, "Negritude and African Humanism," quoted in Bell, *Understanding African Philosophy*, 39.
26. For a detailed explanation of this point, see Manthia Diawara, *In Search of Africa* (Cambridge, MA: Harvard University Press, 1988), 63.
27. See "Tradition and Industrialization," in Wright, *Black Power*, 699–729.
28. Wright, 80.
29. Wright, 101.
30. Wright, 119.
31. Wright, 157.
32. Wright, 241.
33. Wright, 318.
34. Paul Gilroy sees *Black Power* as a classic text in the black Atlantic tradition, especially because Wright's "skeptical views of the value of the premodern can be glimpsed periodically in the work of the other writers, artists, and cultural activists whose work this book has cited or examined. But their distaste for the 'mumbo jumbo' of traditional societies is complex and contradictory." See Gilroy, *The Black Atlantic: Modernity and Double Consciousness* (Cambridge, MA: Harvard University Press, 1995), 192.
35. Richard Wright, *12 Million Black Voices* (New York: Basic, 2002).
36. Wright, *Black Power*, 410.
37. Wright, 415.
38. Wright, 184.
39. Wright, 11.
40. Though Kevin Gaines is correct that Wright's use of militarization had different connotations in the 1950s than it does today—as it was "a major catalyst for black modernity in that it acquainted black peoples with the wider world and facilitated contact with other African-descended peoples"—the concluding letter to Nkrumah expressed a larger suspicion of popular rule that was articulated throughout the text. Gaines, "Revisiting Richard Wright in Ghana," 83.
41. For a more detailed reading of *The Color Curtain*, see Dohra Ahmad, *Landscapes of Hope: Anti-Colonial Utopianism in America* (New York: Oxford University Press, 2009), 180.
42. Richard Wright, *Native Son* (New York: Harper and Row, 1940).

6. SUN RA AND COSMIC BLACKNESS

1. Most scholarly accounts of Ra to date try to situate him in the tradition of black aesthetics or culture, but none examines the way he expresses a meditation on political ideas. For the best accounts of his life, see John Szwed, *Space Is the Place: The Life and Times of Sun Ra* (New York: Da Capo, 1998); and Graham Lock, *Blutopia: Visions of the Future and Revisions of the Past in the Work of Sun Ra, Duke Ellington, and Anthony Braxton* (Durham: Duke University Press, 2000), 13–77.
2. Quoted in Lock, *Blutopia*, 23.
3. See Friedrich Nietzsche, *On The Genealogy of Morals* (New York: Oxford University Press, 2009).
4. The most sustained attempt to recover Ra's philosophy is Paul Youngquist, *A Pure Solar World: Sun Ra and the Birth of Afrofuturism* (Austin: University of Texas Press, 2016).
5. Quoted in Szwed, *Space Is the Place*, 316.
6. Szwed, 295.
7. Lock, *Blutopia*, 63.
8. Szwed, *Space Is the Place*, 313.
9. For an account of this performance, see Szwed, 313.
10. Sun Ra, "The Delusion Freedom," in *Collected Works*, vol. 1, *Immeasurable Equation*, ed. Adam Abraham (Chandler, AZ: Phaelos, 2005), 16.
11. Lock, *Blutopia*, 18–19.
12. Sun Ra, "Calling Planet Earth," in *Immeasurable Equation*, 5.
13. Sun Ra and the Arkestra, "Nuclear War," New York, *Variety Recording Studies*, 1982.
14. Sun Ra, "My Music Is Words," in *Immeasurable Equation*, xxx.
15. Dieter Buchart, *Jean-Michel Basquiat: Now's the Time* (New York: Prestel, 2015), 152.
16. Gunnar Myrdal, *An American Dilemma: The Negro Problem and Modern Democracy* (New York: Routledge, 1995).
17. Szwed, *Space Is the Place*, 313.
18. Szwed, 313.
19. Sun Ra, "Unseen Definitions," in *Immeasurable Equation*, 206.
20. Szwed, *Space Is the Place*, 310.
21. Szwed, 316.
22. Sun Ra, "My Music Is Words," xxix.
23. Szwed, *Space Is the Place*, 242.
24. Sun Ra, "Message to Black Youth," in *Immeasurable Equation*, 79; Sun Ra, "My Music Is Words," xxix.

25. Sun Ra, "My Music Is Words," xxix.
26. Sun Ra, "Other Gods Have I Heard Of" (1972), in *Immeasurable Equation*, 116.
27. Sun Ra, "The Other Otherness" (1972), in *Immeasurable Equation*, 118.
28. Szwed, *Space Is the Place*, 243.
29. Sun Ra, "Points of the Space Age," in *Immeasurable Equation*, 139.

7. SAMUEL DELANY AND THE AMBIGUITY OF UTOPIA

1. David Golumbia, "Black and White World: Race, Ideology, and Utopia in 'Triton' and 'Star Trek,'" *Cultural Critique* 32 (Winter 1995–96): 75–95. As he writes, "It is in this respect that the notion of utopia not as a projection of future social hopes but rather as a doubled reflection of our own society and the forms of its ideology-emerges" (79).
2. The literary critic Tom Moylan has called *Triton* a "critical utopia" in his classic study *Demand the Impossible: Science Fiction and the Utopian Imagination* (New York: Peter Lang, 2014), 149–86.
3. Samuel R. Delany, *Silent Interviews: On Language, Race, Sex, Science Fiction, and Some Comics* (Hanover, NH: Wesleyan Press, 1994), 41.
4. Delany, 134.
5. Samuel Delany, "On 'Triton' and Other Matters: An Interview with Samuel R. Delany," *Science Fiction Studies* 17, no. 3 (November 1990): 303.
6. Delany, *Silent Interviews*, 134.
7. Herbert Marcuse, *Eros and Civilization: A Philosophical Inquiry Into Freud* (Boston: Beacon, 1974).
8. Samuel R. Delany, *Triton* (New York: Bantam, 1976), 6.
9. Delany, 90.
10. Delany, 5.
11. *Triton*'s organizing theory of dichotomizing reality and creating bounded spheres of knowledge resembled the philosophical positivism of the early-twentieth-century Vienna Circle of Moritz Schlick and Rudolph Carnap.
12. Delany, *Triton*, 268.
13. Delany, *Silent Interviews*, 8.
14. Delany, *Triton*, 56.
15. Delany, 254.
16. Delany, 122.
17. Delany, *Silent Interviews*, 59.

18. For an expansion of this, see Robert Elliot Fox, "The Politics of Desire in Delany's Triton and The Tides of Lust," *Black American Literature Forum* 18, no. 2, science fiction issue (Summer 1984): 49–56. As Fox writes, "One of Triton's persistent themes, in fact, is the torment that confusion may generate amid a plenitude of possibilities. Bron hates those who know what they want, because anyone can have their desire (which marks him as an elitist, as does his insistent portrayal of himself as a unique individual in a society in which he is constantly reminded there are only types)" (49).
19. Delany, *Triton*, 302.
20. Delany, 253, 257.
21. Delany, *Silent Interviews*, 178.
22. Delany, *Triton*, 311.
23. Delany, *Silent Interviews*, 115.
24. Delany, *Triton*, 212.
25. Delany, 329–30.

8. OCTAVIA BUTLER AND THE POLITICS OF UTOPIAN TRANSCENDENCE

1. For a summary of the end of the utopia on the left, see Russell Jacoby, *The End of Utopia: Politics and Culture in an Age of Apathy* (New York: Basic, 2000); Francis Fukuyama, *The End of History and the Last Man* (New York: Free, 1992).
2. Ralph Ellison, *Invisible Man* (New York: Vintage, 1995), 1.
3. See Marlene D. Allen, "Octavia Butler's 'Parable' Novels and the 'Boomerang' of African American History," *Callaloo* 32, no. 4, Middle Eastern and North African writers (Winter 2009): 1353–65.
4. While Butler's works have been widely discussed by literary critics over the past few decades, there is only one major full-length study of her life and work. See Gerry Canavan, *Octavia E. Butler* (Urbana: University of Illinois Press, 2016). Among one of the few attempts to read a dystopian and utopian strain in Butler's Parable books is Jim Miller, "Post-Apocalyptic Hoping: Octavia Butler's Dystopian/Utopian Vision," *Science Fiction Studies* 25, no. 2 (July 1998): 336–60. Miller's objective, however, is to read the text within the backdrop of US cultural production—or as a cultural response to existing politics—but my goal throughout this chapter is to read the books as utopian political theory.

5. This bore striking resemblances to Democratic president Bill Clinton's agreement with a reactionary Republican Congress to "end welfare as we know it" in 1996.
6. Butler, *Parable of the Sower* (New York: Seven Stories, 1993), 27.
7. Butler, 10.
8. The idea that community was being eroded by a lack of civic trust came, most prominently, from Robert Putnam, *Bowling Alone: The Collapse and Revival of American Community* (New York: Touchstone, 2001).
9. *Parable* extended Margaret Atwood's critique in *The Handmaid's Tale* (1986) of the assault on women's reproductive rights and freedom inaugurated by the religious fundamentalism of the Reagan administration in the 1980s.
10. Butler, *Parable of the Sower*, 57.
11. Butler, 20.
12. Butler, 80.
13. Butler, *Parable of the Talents* (New York: Seven Stories, 1998), 281.
14. Butler, *Parable of the Sower*, 2.
15. Butler, 135.
16. See Nietzsche, *On The Genealogy of Morals* (New York: Oxford University Press, 2009).
17. Butler, *Parable of the Sower*, 47.
18. Butler, 29.
19. Butler, 171.

CONCLUSION

1. Karl Popper, *The Open Society and Its Enemies: The Spell of Plato* (Princeton: Princeton University Press, 1971), 159.
2. Addressing the charge of utopia's connection to totalitarianism is something almost all contemporary commentators do. And yet, as Russell Jacoby rightly claims, it is mistaken to uncritically charge utopia as somehow being intrinsically violent. After all, even if one might argue that utopia—as the dream for an ideal society—has a political history in the twentieth century with Nazism and Stalinism, the intellectual history of utopia is radically different. As Jacoby importantly writes, "Any study of the utopian spirit must engage its current status. . . . I contest the notion that Nazi ideologues belong in this company. The Nazi preoccupation with racial purity, war, and genocide shares nothing with

classic utopian motifs." Russell Jacoby, *Picture Imperfect: Utopian Thought for an Anti-Utopian Age* (New York: Columbia University Press, 2005), x. Still, there has been a recent resurgence in such thinking, especially through the new academic journal, *Utopian Studies*.

3. Russell Jacoby, *The End of Utopia: Politics and Culture in an Age of Apathy* (New York: Basic, 2000), xii.
4. Lewis Mumford makes the convincing argument that utopian ideas and the architecture of the city have been deeply intertwined since antiquity. See Lewis Mumford, *The Story of Utopias* (New York: Liveright, 1922).
5. Judith Shklar, "The Political Theory of Utopia: From Melancholy to Nostalgia," in *Utopias and Utopian Thought*, ed. Frank E. Manuel (Boston: Beacon, 1967), 105.
6. See Emma Goldman, *Red Emma Speaks: An Emma Goldman Reader*, ed. Alix Kate Shulman (Amherst: Humanity, 1972), 63–64.
7. Sigmund Freud, *The Interpretation of Dreams*, trans. James Strachey (New York: Basic, 2010).
8. Part of my argument is that utopia can be used as a method for thinking through contemporary politics. Here I am following Ruth Levitas, who argues that "a utopian method relevant to the twenty-first century . . . provides a critical tool for exposing the limitations of current policy discourses about economic growth and ecological sustainability. It facilitates genuinely holistic thinking about possible futures, combined with reflexivity, provisionality and democratic engagement with the principles and practice of those futures." See Ruth Levitas, *Utopia as Method: The Imaginary Reconstitution of Society* (New York: Palgrave Macmillan, 2013), xi.
9. Paul Tillich, "Critique and Justification of Utopia," in Manuel, *Utopias and Utopian Thought*, 309.
10. Jürgen Habermas, *Between Facts and Norms: Contributions to a Discourse Theory of Law and Democracy* (Cambridge, MA: MIT Press, 1998).
11. See also Imani Perry, *More Beautiful and More Terrible: The Embrace and Transcendence of Racial Inequality in American* (New York: New York University Press, 2011); David Roediger, *The Wages of Whiteness: Race and the Making of the American Working Class* (New York: Verso, 2007).
12. At times, their work exemplifies the French philosopher Jean-Luc Nancy's argument that myths of organic community are false, that communities are always incomplete. See Jean-Luc Nancy, *The Inoperative Community* (Minneapolis: University of Minnesota Press, 1991).

13. For an expression and critique of this view, see Desmond S. King and Rogers Smith, *Still a House Divided: Race and Politics in Obama's America* (Princeton: Princeton University Press, 2013).
14. See Corey Robin, *Fear: The History of a Political Idea* (New York: Oxford University Press, 2006).
15. For an excellent account of the way disaster precludes political responsibility, see Jane Anna Gordon and Lewis Gordon, *Of Divine Warning: Disaster in a Modern Age* (New York: Routledge, 2016).
16. For a contemporary account of Afro-pessimism, see Frank Wilderson, *Red, White and Black: Cinema and the Structure of US Antagonisms* (Durham: Duke University Press, 2010); for a critical kind of Afro-optimism, see Joseph R. Winters, *Hope Draped in Black: Race, Melancholy, and the Agony of Racial Progress* (Durham: Duke University Press, 2016).
17. This American tradition is most clearly expressed by James Madison, "Federalist no. 10," in *The Federalist*, ed. Terence Ball (Cambridge: Cambridge University Press, 2003), 40–46.
18. Black utopian thought demonstrates what Neil Roberts calls the idea of freedom as marronage in *Freedom as Marronage* (Chicago: University of Chicago Press, 2015).
19. In this sense, they are in dialogue with Hannah Arendt's critique of the traditional conception of modern power, developed by Thomas Hobbes, which asserted that power and violence were linked. But while Arendt argues that power should be recast as action in concert and violence should be rejected because of its instrumental character, she inadequately explains the way that the oppressed find power in unexpected moments like critical judgment or countercultural activities—not simply through collective political action. For Arendt's critique, see Hannah Arendt, *On Violence* (New York: Harvest, 1970).

BIBLIOGRAPHY

Adekele, Tunde. *Without Regard to Race: The Other Martin Robison Delany*. Jackson: University Press of Mississippi, 2009.

Adorno, Theodor. *Minima Moralia: Reflections on a Damaged Life*. New York: Verso, 2006.

Adorno, Theodor, and Max Horkheimer. *Dialectic of Enlightenment*. Palo Alto: Stanford University Press, 2007.

Ahmad, Dora. *Landscapes of Hope: Anti-Colonial Utopianism in America*. New York: Oxford University Press, 2009.

Allen, Danielle S. *Talking to Strangers: Anxieties of Citizenship After Brown v. Board of Education*. Chicago: University of Chicago Press, 2004.

Allen, Marlene D. "Octavia Butler's 'Parable' Novels and the 'Boomerang' of African American History." *Callaloo* 32, no. 4, Middle Eastern and North African Writers (Winter 2009): 1353–65.

Arendt, Hannah. *The Human Condition*. Chicago: University of Chicago Press, 1958.

——. *On Revolution*. New York: Penguin, 2006.

——. *On Violence*. New York: Harvest, 1970.

Bain, Alexander M. "Shocks Americana: George Schuyler Serializes Black Internationalism." *American Literary History* 19, no. 4 (Winter 2007): 937–63.

Balfour, Lawrie. *Democracy's Reconstruction: Thinking Politically with W. E. B. Du Bois*. New York: Oxford University Press, 2011.

Bell, Richard. *Understanding African Philosophy*. New York: Routledge, 2002.

Bloch, Ernst. *The Spirit of Utopia*. Palo Alto: Stanford University Press, 2000.

Bogues, Anthony. *Black Heretics, Black Prophets: Radical Political Intellectuals*. New York: Routledge, 2003.

Boyd, Melba J. *Discarded Legacy: Politics and Poetics in the Life of Frances E. W. Harper, 1825–1911*. Detroit: Wayne State University Press, 1994.

Bromell, Nick. *The Time Is Always Now: Black Thought and the Transformation of US Democracy*. New York: Oxford University Press, 2013.

Buchart, Dieter. *Jean-Michel Basquiat: Now's the Time*. New York: Prestel, 2015.

Buck-Morss, Susan. *Dreamworld and Catastrophe: The Passing of Mass Utopia in East and West*. Cambridge, MA: MIT Press, 2002.

Butler, Octavia E. *Parable of the Sower*. New York: Seven Stories, 1993.

——. *Parable of the Talents*. New York: Seven Stories, 1998.

Canavan, Gerry. *Octavia E. Butler*. Urbana: University of Illinois Press, 2016.

Carby, Hazel V. *The Magazine Novels of Pauline Hopkins*. Edited by Henry Louis Gates, Jr. Oxford: Oxford University Press, 1988.

——. *Race Men*. Cambridge, MA: Harvard University Press, 2000.

——. *Reconstructing Womanhood: The Emergence of the Afro-American Woman Novelist*. New York: Oxford University Press, 1989.

Chakkalal, Tess, and Kenneth Warren, eds. *Jim Crow, Literature, and the Legacy of Sutton E. Griggs*. Athens: University of Georgia Press, 2013.

Chrostowska, S. D., and James D. Ingram, eds. *Political Uses of Utopia: New Marxist, Anarchist, and Radical Democratic Perspectives*. New York: Columbia University Press, 2016.

Cooper, Anna Julia. *A Voice From the South* (1892), http://docsouth.unc.edu/church/cooper/cooper.html.

Dawson, Michael C. *Black Visions: The Roots of Contemporary African-American Political Ideologies*. Chicago: University of Chicago Press, 2001.

Delany, Martin. *Blake; or the Huts of America*. Cambridge, MA: Harvard University Press, 2017.

——. *The Condition, Elevation, Emigration and Destiny of the Colored People of the United States*. Baltimore: Black Classic, 1991.

——. *The Official Report of the Niger Valley Expedition* (1861), www.gutenberg.org/files/22118/22118-h/22118-h.htm.

——. *Principa of Ethnology: The Origins of the Races and Color*. Philadelphia: Harper and Brothers, 1880.

Delany, Samuel. "On 'Triton' and Other Matters: An Interview with Samuel R. Delany." *Science Fiction Studies* 17, no. 3 (November 1990): 295–324.

——. *Silent Interviews: On Language, Race, Sex, Science Fiction, and Some Comics*. Hanover, NH: Wesleyan University Press, 1994.

——. *Triton*. New York: Bantam, 1976.

Dery, Mark. *Flame Wars: The Discourse of Cyberculture*. Durham: Duke University Press, 1994.

Diawara, Manthia. *In Search of Africa*. Cambridge, MA: Harvard University Press, 1988.

Du Bois, W. E. B. *Dark Princess*. Jackson: University Press of Mississippi, 1995.

——. *Darkwater: Voices From Within the Veil.* New York: Dover, 2009.

Ellison, Ralph. *Invisible Man.* New York: Vintage, 1995.

Emerson, Ralph Waldo. *Political Writings.* Cambridge: Cambridge University Press, 2008.

Eyerman, Ron. *Cultural Trauma: Slavery and the Formation of African American Identity.* Cambridge: Cambridge University Press, 2002.

Fabi, Giula. *Passing and the Rise of the African American Novel.* Urbana: University of Illinois Press, 2001.

Fabre, Michel. *The World of Richard Wright.* Jackson: University of Mississippi Press, 1985.

Fanon, Frantz. *The Wretched of the Earth.* New York: Grove, 2005.

Ferguson, Jeffrey B. *The Sage of Sugar Hill: George S. Schuyler and the Harlem Renaissance.* New Haven: Yale University Press, 2008.

Fox, Robert Elliot. "The Politics of Desire in Delany's Triton and The Tides of Lust." *Black American Literature Forum* 18, no. 2, science fiction issue (Summer 1984): 49–56.

Franklin, Benjamin. *Autobiography, and Other Writings.* Edited by Ormond Seavey. Oxford: Oxford University Press, 2008.

Frederickson, George. *Racism: A Short History.* Princeton: Princeton University Press, 2009.

Freud, Sigmund. *The Interpretation of Dreams.* Translated by James Strachey. New York: Basic, 2010.

Fukuyama, Francis. *The End of History and the Last Man.* New York: Free, 1992.

Gaines, Kevin. *African Americans in Ghana: Black Expatriates and the Civil Rights Era.* Chapel Hall: University of North Carolina Press, 2008.

——. "Revisiting Richard Wright in Ghana: Black Radicalism and the Dialectics of Diaspora." *Social Text* 67, vol. 19, no. 2 (Summer 2001): 75–101.

Gilman, Susan. *Blood Talk: American Race Melodrama and the Culture of the Occult.* Chicago: University of Chicago Press, 2003.

Gilroy, Paul. *The Black Atlantic: Modernity and Double Consciousness.* Cambridge, MA: Harvard University Press, 1995.

Glaude, Eddie. *Exodus! Religion, Race and Nation in Early Nineteenth-Century Black America.* Chicago: University of Chicago Press, 2000.

Goldman, Emma. *Red Emma Speaks: An Emma Goldman Reader.* Edited by Alix Kate Shulman. Amherst: Humanity, 1972.

Golumbia, David. "Black and White World: Race, Ideology, and Utopia in 'Triton' and 'Star Trek.'" *Cultural Critique* 32 (Winter 1995–96): 75–95.

Gordon, Jane. *Creolizing Political Theory: Reading Rousseau Through Fanon.* New York: Fordham University Press, 2014.

Gordon, Jane Anna, and Lewis Gordon. *Of Divine Warning: Disaster in a Modern Age*. New York: Routledge, 2016.
Gordon, Lewis R. *An Introduction to Africana Philosophy*. New York: Cambridge University Press, 2008.
Griggs, Sutton E. *Imperium in Imperio*. New York: Modern Library, 2004.
Habermas, Jürgen. *Between Facts and Norms: Contributions to a Discourse Theory of Law and Democracy*. Cambridge, MA: MIT Press, 1998.
——. *The Structural Transformation of the Public Sphere: An Inquiry Into a Category of Bourgeois Society*. Cambridge, MA: MIT Press, 1991.
Harper, Frances. *Iola Leroy; Or, Shadows Uplifted*. New York: Dover, 2010.
Hegel, G. W. F. *Lectures on the Philosophy of World History*. Translated by H. B. Nisbet. Cambridge: Cambridge University Press, 1975.
——. *The Phenomenology of Spirit*. Translated by A. V. Miller. New York: Oxford University Press, 1977.
Henry, Paget. *Caliban's Reason: Introducing Afro-Caribbean Philosophy*. New York: Routledge, 2000.
Higgins, Nathan Irvin. *The Harlem Renaissance*. New York: Oxford University Press, 1972.
Hooker, Juliet. *Theorizing Race in the Americas: Douglass, Sarmiento, Du Bois, and Vasconcelos*. New York: Oxford University Press, 2017.
Hopkins, Pauline. *Of One Blood; or The Hidden Self*. New York: Washington Square, 2004.
Iton, Richard. *In Search of the Black Fantastic: Politics and Popular Culture in the Post–Civil Rights Era*. New York: Oxford University Press, 2011.
Jackson, Walter A. *Gunnar Myrdal and America's Conscience: Social Engineering and American Liberalism, 1938–1987*. Chapel Hill: University of North Carolina Press, 1990.
Jacoby, Russell. *The End of Utopia: Politics and Culture in an Age of Apathy*. New York: Basic, 2000.
——. *Picture Imperfect: Utopian Thought for an Anti-Utopian Age*. New York: Columbia University Press, 2005.
Jarrett, Gene Andrew. *Representing the Race: A New Political History of African American Literature*. New York: New York University Press, 2011.
Jefferson, Thomas. *Notes on the State of Virginia*. Boston: Lily and Wait, 1832.
Jennings, Chris. *Paradise Now: The Story of American Utopianism*. New York: Random House, 2016.
Johnson, Edward A. *Light Ahead for the Negro*. New York: Grafton, 1904.
Kateb, George. *Utopia and Its Enemies*. New York: Free Press of Glencoe, 1963.
Kazin, Michael. *The Populist Persuasion: An American History*. Ithaca: Cornell University Press, 1998.

Kelley, Robin D. G. *Freedom Dreams: The Black Radical Imagination*. Boston: Beacon, 2003.

King, Desmond S., and Rogers Smith. *Still a House Divided: Race and Politics in Obama's America*. Princeton: Princeton University Press, 2013.

Lasky, Melvin. *Utopia and Revolution*. Chicago: University of Chicago Press, 1976.

Lebron, Christopher. *The Making of Black Lives Matter: A Brief History of an Idea*. New York: Oxford University Press, 2017.

Levering-Lewis, David. *W. E. B. Du Bois: A Biography, 1868–1863*. New York: Holt, 2009.

Levinas, Emanuel. *Totality and Infinity: An Essay on Exteriority*. Pittsburgh: Duquesne University Press, 1969.

Levine, Robert. *Martin Delany, Frederick Douglass, and the Politics of Representative Identity*. Chapel Hill: University of North Carolina Press, 1997.

Levitas, Ruth. *Utopia as Method: The Imaginary Reconstitution of Society*. New York: Palgrave Macmillan, 2013.

Lock, Graham. *Blutopia: Visions of the Future and Revisions of the Past in the Work of Sun Ra, Duke Ellington, and Anthony Braxton*. Durham: Duke University Press, 2000.

Madison, James, Alexander Hamilton, and John Jay. *The Federalist*. Edited by Terence Ball. Cambridge: Cambridge University Press, 2003.

Mannheim, Karl. *Ideology and Utopia: Introduction to the Sociology of Knowledge*. New York: Harvest, 1965.

Manuel, Frank E., ed. *Utopias and Utopian Thought*. Boston: Beacon, 1967.

Manuel, Frank E., and Fritzie P. Manuel. *Utopian Thought in the Western World*. Cambridge, MA: Belknap Press of Harvard University Press, 1979.

Marcuse, Herbert. *Eros and Civilization: A Philosophical Inquiry Into Freud*. Boston: Beacon, 1974.

Marx, Karl, and Friedrich Engels. *The Marx-Engels Reader*. Edited by Robert C. Tucker. New York: Norton, 1978.

McKnight, Utz. *Race and the Politics of Exception: Equality, Sovereignty and American Democracy*. New York: Routledge, 2013.

Miller, Jim. "Post-Apocalyptic Hoping: Octavia Butler's Dystopian/Utopian Vision." *Science Fiction Studies* 25, no. 2 (July 1998): 336–60.

Mills, Charles. *From Class to Race: Essays in White Marxism and Black Radicalism*. Lanham, MD: Rowman and Littlefield, 2003.

Moses, Wilson J. *Afrotopia: The Roots of African American Popular History*. New York: Cambridge University Press, 1998.

Moses, Wilson J. *Creative Conflict in African American Thought*. Cambridge: Cambridge University Press, 2004.

——. *The Golden Age of Black Nationalism, 1850–1925*. New York: Oxford University Press, 1988.

Moylan, Tom. *Demand the Impossible: Science Fiction and the Utopian Imagination*. New York: Peter Lang, 2014.

Mumford, Lewis. *The Story of Utopias*. New York: Liveright, 1922.

Myrdal, Gunnar. *An American Dilemma: The Negro Problem and Modern Democracy*. New York: Routledge, 1995.

Nancy, Jean-Luc. *The Inoperative Community*. Minneapolis: University of Minnesota Press, 1991.

Nietzsche, Friedrich. *The Gay Science*. New York: Vintage, 2010.

——. *On The Genealogy of Morals*. New York: Oxford University Press, 2009.

Painter, Nell Irvin. "Martin Delany: Elitism and Black Nationalism." In *Black Leaders of the Nineteenth Century*, edited by Leon Litwack and August Meier. Urbana: University of Illinois Press, 1991.

Pease, William H., and Jane Pease. *Black Utopia: Negro Communal Experiments in America*. Madison: State Historical Society of Wisconsin, 1963.

Perry, Imani. *More Beautiful and More Terrible: The Embrace and Transcendence of Racial Inequality in American*. New York: New York University Press, 2011.

Pfeifer, Michael J. *Rough Justice: Lynching and American Society, 1874–1947*. Urbana: University of Illinois Press, 2004.

Polak, Fred. *The Image of the Future*. New York: Elsevier, 1973.

Popper, Karl. *The Open Society and Its Enemies: The Spell of Plato*. Princeton: Princeton University Press, 1971.

Pratt, Mary Louise. *Imperial Eyes: Travel Writing and Transculturation*. New York: Routledge, 2007.

Putnam, Robert. *Bowling Alone: The Collapse and Revival of American Community*. New York: Touchstone, 2001.

Ra, Sun. *Collected Works*. Vol. 1, *Immeasurable Equation*. Edited by Adam Abraham. Chandler, AZ: Phaelos, 2005.

Ra, Sun, and the Arkestra. "Nuclear War." *Variety Recording Studies*. New York, 1982.

Rabaka, Rieland. "WEB Dubois's 'The Comet' and Contributions to Critical Race Theory: An Essay on Black Radical Politics and Anti-Racist Social Ethics." *Ethnic Studies Review* 29, no. 1:36–59.

Reed, Adolph. *W. E. B. Du Bois and American Political Thought: Fabianism and the Color Line*. New York: Oxford University Press, 1999.

Retman, Sonnet. "Black No More: George Schuyler and Racial Capitalism." *PMLA* 123, no. 5 (October 2008): 1448–64.

Rhodes, Harold V. *Utopia in American Political Thought.* Tucson: University of Arizona Press, 1967.

Roberts, Neil. *Freedom as Marronage.* Chicago: University of Chicago Press, 2015.

Robin, Corey. *Fear: The History of a Political Idea.* New York: Oxford University Press, 2006.

Robinson, Cedric J. *Black Marxism: The Making of the Black Radical Tradition.* Chapel Hill: University of North Carolina Press, 2000.

Roediger, David. *The Wages of Whiteness: Race and the Making of the American Working Class.* New York: Verso, 2007.

Rowley, Hazel. *Richard Wright: The Life and Times.* Chicago: University of Chicago Press, 2008.

Sargent, Lyman Tower. *Utopianism: A Very Short Introduction.* New York: Oxford University Press, 2010.

Schuyler, George S. *Black Empire.* Boston: Northeastern University Press, 1993.

——. *Black No More: Being an Account of Strange and Wonderful Workings of Science in the Land of the Free, A.D. 1933–1940.* New York: Modern Library, 1999.

Scott, James C. *Domination and the Arts of Resistance: Hidden Transcripts.* New Haven: Yale University Press, 1993.

Shelby, Tommie. "Two Conceptions of Black Nationalism: Martin Delany on the Meaning of Black Solidarity." *Political Theory* 31, no. 5 (2003): 664–92.

Sterling, Dorothy. *The Making of an Afro-American: Martin Robison Delany, 1812–1885.* Garden City, NY: Da Capo, 1971.

Stringer, Dorothy. "Psychology and Black Liberation in Richard Wright's Black Power." *Journal of Modern Literature* 32, no. 4 (Summer 2009): 105–24.

Stuckey, Sterling. *The Ideological Origins of Black Nationalism.* Boston: Beacon, 1972.

Sundquist, Eric J. *To Wake the Nations: Race in the Making of American Literature.* Cambridge, MA: Harvard University Press, 1993.

Sundstrom, Ronald R. "The Prophetic and Pragmatic Philosophy of 'Race' in WEB Du Bois's 'The Comet.'" *APA Newsletter on Philosophy and the Black Experience* 99, no. 1 (Fall 1999).

Szwed, John. *Space Is the Place: The Life and Times of Sun Ra.* New York: Da Capo, 1998.

Turner, Jack. *Awakening to Race: Individualism and Social Consciousness in America.* Chicago: University of Chicago Press, 2012.

Ullman, Victor. *Martin Delany: The Beginnings of Black Nationalism.* Boston: Beacon, 1971.

Wallinger, Hanna. *Pauline Hopkins: A Literary Biography.* Athens: University of Georgia Press, 2012.

Warren, Kenneth W. "An Inevitable Drift? Oligarchy, Du Bois, and the Politics of Race Between the Wars." *Boundary 2* 27, no. 3 (Fall 2000): 153–69.

Washington, Mary Helen. *The Other Blacklist: The African American Literary and Cultural Left of the 1950s.* New York: Columbia University Press, 2013.

Weber, Max. *The Protestant Ethic and the Spirit of Capitalism.* New York: Routledge, 2001.

Wiebe, Robert. *The Search for Order, 1877–1920.* New York: Hill and Wang, 1967.

Wilderson, Frank. *Red, White and Black: Cinema and the Structure of US Antagonisms.* Durham: Duke University Press, 2010.

Winters, Joseph R. *Hope Draped in Black: Race, Melancholy, and the Agony of Racial Progress.* Durham: Duke University Press, 2016.

Wolin, Sheldon. *Politics and Vision: Continuity and Innovation in Western Political Thought.* Princeton: Princeton University Press, 2016.

Wright, Richard. *12 Million Black Voices.* New York: Basic, 2002.

——. *Black Power.* New York: Vintage, 2008.

——. *Native Son.* New York: Harper and Row, 1940.

X, Malcolm. *By Any Means Necessary.* New York: Pathfinder, 1992.

Youngquist, Paul. *A Pure Solar World: Sun Ra and the Birth of Afrofuturism.* Austin: University of Texas Press, 2016.

Zamalin, Alex. *African American Political Thought and American Culture: The Nation's Struggle for Racial Justice.* New York: Palgrave Macmillan, 2015.

——. *Struggle on Their Minds: The Political Thought of African American Resistance.* New York: Columbia University Press, 2017.

INDEX